Buyer Attitudes and Brand Choice Behavior

GRADUATE SCHOOL OF BUSINESS DISSERTATIONS SERIES
Columbia University and The Free Press

L. R. Burgess, *Top Executive Pay Package*
P. O. Dietz, *Pensions Funds: Measuring Investment Performance*
T. C. Gaines, *Techniques of Treasury Debt Management*
B. Yavitz, *Automation in Commercial Banking: Its Process and Impact*

Buyer Attitudes and Brand Choice Behavior

GEORGE S. DAY

THE FREE PRESS, NEW YORK
COLLIER-MACMILLAN LIMITED, LONDON

Contents

List of Tables

List of Illustrations

Preface

> . . . attitudes are always seen as precursors of behavior, as deter-
> minants of how a person will actually behave in his daily affairs.
>
> —*Arthur R. Cohen*

The above statement has "face" validity for most marketing
researchers and decision makers. On the strength of statements
such as this and the undeniable logical appeal of attitudes' serving
as predictors of brand choice behavior, attitude surveys have
become an important marketing decision tool. From the results of
countless attitude surveys come inferences about the success of
new products, the effectiveness of changes in the marketing mix,
and the worth of major advertising campaigns. Ever increasing
emphasis is being placed on attitude measures to pre-test advertising copy and to screen new product concepts.

According to George Brown (1950), the main reason for any
early lack of interest in attitudes toward brands was the seeming
success of the continuous purchase panel and the store audit in
diagnosing marketing problems. However, as is so often the case,
the reduction of the executive's uncertainty in the area of price,
distribution, and the like merely highlighted his lack of understanding of the preference and knowledge structure of the market.
The increasing dependence on attitude surveys, as an additional
control device, coincided with a noticeable shortening of the life

cycle of many consumer products (Berg and Shuchman, 1963). Consequently, when faced with the need to develop and appraise a large number of new product concepts, many research executives turned to economical and insightful attitude surveys for guidance. This is true today in even the most advanced product development systems (Stefflre, 1965). Other problem areas in marketing have similarly benefited from the recognition that recourse to buyer attitudes is the most direct way to understand observed purchase patterns.

Underlying this growing reliance on the measurement of brand attitudes is an apparent contradiction which confronts many of the most enthusiastic users. As we noted at the outset, most marketers feel that brand attitudes "should" predict subsequent behavior. Yet many of these same people harbor serious doubts about the ability of their instruments to tap the appropriate attitudes and are not at all certain about the strength and nature of the predictive relationship. Both of these doubts were, for a time, partly assuaged by cross-section surveys, which rather consistently found that favorable attitudes toward a brand were associated with a high probability of a *recent* purchase of that brand. This was encouraging; but of course it said little about future behavior over a sequence of purchases, and it was contaminated by the tendency for survey respondents to ensure consistency between attitude and behavior responses given at the same point in time. Recently, however, theoretical and methodological advances by the behavioral sciences have made possible much deeper insights into the complexity of the relationship, and most of all into the numerous potential sources of error. There is little justification for complacency in many of their conclusions about the difficulty of obtaining reliable and valid attitudes; and there is a profound warning in the repeated finding that acceptable aggregate predictions are often achieved from very poor predictions of individual behavior. This evidence is presently being assimilated in marketing and creating considerable anxiety in the process. Clearly if attitudes do not say something about behavior, then their diagnostic value is very limited. Meanwhile there are increasing demands on attitude measurement as brand differences become more subtle, advertising remains as hard to evaluate as ever, and an emerging body of marketing theory looks to attitudes as a central integrating feature.

Despite the apparent need to understand the predictive value of brand attitudes, there is a large gap between what we presently know and what we should know. This study is directed toward closing this gap.

The Scope of the Study

The attack on the problem of the predictive value of brand attitudes will be made in two distinct, though closely related, stages. The first stage is concerned with *describing* the predictive relationship of brand attitudes with subsequent brand choice behavior. Unfortunately, description does not usually confer cumulative understanding, however important it may be for specific evaluation problems. So, rather than stopping at this point, we will also look at the various influences on behavior in addition to attitudes. This second stage will be guided by an interpretive model of the relationship which accounts for the two major sources of discrepancy between attitudes and behavior: first, that the constraints and opportunities of the environment at the time of purchase are not represented in the attitude measure; and second, that the usual concept of attitude (as well as the associated attitude measures) does not consider all the sources of individual variability in the strength of motives that guide behavior. This model does not depend on any assumptions about the nature of attitudes (or attitude change) as either *causing* subsequent behavior (or behavior change) or merely *reflecting* earlier experience with the product class. In essence we are seeking to explain the relationship of attitudes to subsequent behavior, rather than the source of the attitudes.

In Chapter 1 we try to avoid "reinventing the wheel" by reviewing the results of other investigations into the general problem area—particularly studies dealing with voting behavior, consumer intentions to buy, and buying behavior. From this we can draw some tentative conclusions about the kind of relationship to expect and the influences to take into account. Also, we are able to derive certain standards which any study must satisfy if it is to explore the problem successfully.

The interpretive model used to guide this study is developed in Chapter 2. Its starting point is the theoretical position that observed brand attitudes and related choice behavior represent the evaluative and behavioral manifestations of a single underlying or latent structure. However, these two manifestations take place under different and changing environments, and at different times. This means that, during the period in which behavior is being studied, there are many opportunities for temporary disruptions or even permanent change in latent structure. In the model these possibilities are treated as part of a learning process that dampens behavior, so it is never as extreme as the initial attitude would indicate. The extent of damping depends not only on the initial attitude, but also on the stability of the latent structure and the individual's buying style—that is, his characteristic response to the purchasing environment. Both stability and buying style are explicitly incorporated in the model as factors that contribute to (or detract from) the strength of the predictive relationship. Throughout this study we will refer to them as *moderating effects*: a term originally used to refer to error-producing effects, but equally relevant in this context.

Chapter 3 elaborates the model by describing the environmental influences of exposure to new information, the competitive effect of similar brands, and various interferences such as price, lack of availability, time pressure, overall financial constraints, and the influence of family decision processes. In most cases enough is known about these environmental influences to make it feasible to appraise the nature and direction of their influence. Less is known about the moderating effects of stability and buying style, as well as unpredictable desires to change, or response biases, because these effects lead to inconsistent and potentially unpredictable behavior.

Chapters 4 and 5 are the empirical analogues of Chapters 2 and 3. That is, we first look at the attitude-subsequent behavior relationship per se and then study the specific environmental influences and moderating effects. Two sets of panel data are used to test the model and isolate the specific influences on the relationship. The first panel contains data on appliances, the second is on a convenience food product. The analysis of the influences on the attitude-subsequent behavior relationship is considerably strengthened by the opportunity to contrast two types of purchase decisions that differ so greatly in importance and length of repurchase cycle.

In Chapter 6 we reappraise the model in light of the findings, draw some implications for the use of brand attitudes as management decision tools, and suggest a number of directions for further work that can build on and improve this endeavor. The model is appraised as an alternative approach to the study of brand loyalty because of an improved capacity to account for the influences that lead to loyal or switching behavior.

This dissertation study was made feasible because of the fortunate availability of two different consumer panels which combined brand attitude and purchase behavior measures with very detailed information on respondent characteristics. Thus my greatest debts are to Mr. Robert W. Pratt, Jr., Manager of the Consumer Behavior Research Program of the General Electric Company, who gave me access to their data and a wealth of research experience, and to the food products manufacturer that collaborated with Professor John Howard in the collection of the non-durables data by the Columbia University Research Program on Buyer Behavior.

However I would not have been sensitive to the possibilities in the data had Professor Howard not introduced me to the problem and its many interesting ramifications. I was also fortunate to have his continuing encouragement and, through him, the opportunity to serve as the project director for the first stage of the Research Program on Buyer Behavior.

Many other people contributed freely of their time and insights and share the credit where it is due. I am particularly indebted to Professor David W. Miller for his continuing support of the model used to organize the analysis, and to Professor Ivar E. Berg, Jr., for contributing a welcome balance to this study. I would be remiss if I did not acknowledge the benefits of my acquaintance with the work of Professors Abraham Shuchman, Jagdish N. Sheth, and William J. McGuire. The evolution of this study into the form in which it appears was aided by many helpful insights and comments from my associates here at Stanford. In particular I am grateful to Michael L. Ray and Henry J. Claycamp. The long process of rethinking and rewriting was only sustainable because of the support and understanding of my wife, Marilyn.

Palo Alto, California   GEORGE S. DAY

Chapter 1

·The Problem and
Some Past Insights

The approach to understanding the predictive power of brand attitudes by looking for systematic influences on the relationship of individual attitudes to over-time choice behavior has a simple appeal. But one immediately wonders whether it has been done before. This feeling is initially reinforced by the truly enormous literature that is devoted to attitude theory and measurement. However, within this literature there appears to be relatively little in the way of systematic consideration of the attitude–subsequent behavior relationship—and even fewer empirical results. Nonetheless, what literature there is has been helpful in illuminating the problems and guiding the analytical model used in this report, and particularly useful in setting the standards that this study should strive to meet. At the end of the chapter we take a different perspective to see what several developing areas of marketing theory and practice should know about the attitude–behavior relationship if they are to achieve their promise.

The Generality of the Problem

Many marketers were forcibly made aware of the state of knowledge in other disciplines by a controversial paper by

Festinger (1964). He was provoked by a statement by Cohen (1964, page 238), which observed that there was little work explicitly dealing with the behavior that results from a new (changed) attitude. Upon looking for such studies, he was "astonished" to find only three that were relevant. The criteria for the relevancy of a study was the application of a design which looked for differences in behavior between a control group and an experimental group whose attitude had been changed by an exposure to a persuasive communication. In other words, do different attitudes predict different behaviors? The three studies, which dealt with toilet training, a human relations course for foremen, and a reinterpretation of the Janis and Fesbach (1953) study on the effects of fear-arousing communications, produced slightly inverse relationships.[1] Festinger concluded that:

> . . . in order to produce a stable behavior change following opinion change, an environmental change must also be produced which, representing reality, will support the new opinion and the new behavior. Otherwise, the same factors that produced the initial opinion and the behavior will continue to operate to nullify the effect of the opinion change.[2]

Students of propaganda (notably Ellul, 1965) have argued the same point: that all the elements of the environment must operate in concert to support and maintain the attitude, otherwise predictive efficacy will be nil. This lesson about the influence of environmental conditions is just as applicable to predictions made with brand attitudes as with any other attitudes.

Festinger did not doubt that attitudes do relate to *relevant* behavior, even though he realized that few studies had addressed the problem. Two of the best known studies, by La Piere and De Fleur and Westie (1958), looked at racial attitudes under different

---

1. A reanalysis of the Janis and Fesbach study by Achenbaum (1966) indicates that Festinger's conclusion may be unfounded. First, the samples were not matched on initial attitude; second, the samples used were relatively small; and third, the only group that did not react as expected received a fear appeal that could have had an ambiguous effect by inhibiting action.

2. 1964, page 416.

2

circumstances.[3] The latter study found that the two extreme groups did behave somewhat differently in a quasi-authentic situation. The La Piere study provides clearer lessons about the meaning of brand attitudes. Essentially, motel keepers who said they would not accept Chinese guests invariably admitted them when they arrived. Many explanations have been offered to explain the extreme disparity. Most of them boil down to the fact that in situations like this, the attitude system (or underlying process) behaves differently depending on the context or situation. For example the underlying attitude may be discriminatory, but the context may dictate that it is better to avoid a painful situation than to express this attitude.

We will encounter the influence of the environment on the behavioral manifestation of attitudes[4] in many guises throughout this report. In every case, however, predictions of behavior from prior attitudes are only feasible when the environment is correctly specified. For example, employee attitudes are only useful as predictors of behavior when the same conditions influence both measures (Vroom, 1964). Thus employee attitudes and absence and turnover rates have correlated (as high as 0.69) because both are related to the relative number and importance of the rewards and punishments provided by the work role. However, because job performance is also affected by "the basis for the attainment of rewards and punishments," it is not associated with employee attitudes at all.

To reinforce the importance of environmental influences on the relationship we turn to two research traditions—voting and the forecasting of durable goods expenditures—which have direct relevance to buying behavior. In fact, some of the recent research on the prediction of partisan choice has goals which are quite similar to the goals of this study.

---

3. There are numerous articles on the discrepancy between racial attitudes and overt behavior. For a recent review see Fendrich (1966).

4. More accurately, as we shall see in Chapter 2, the attitude is really the verbal representation of a latent process, and it is this latent process that is influenced by the environment.

Voting

The similarity between voting and buying decisions has been periodically rediscovered and restated (for example, Burdick and Brodbeck, 1959). In some respects voting is the easier decision to understand, because it is usually confined to one point in time and two or three possible alternatives. Often the decision is accompanied by the same lack of involvement that tends to confound research in buying behavior:

> . . . it is a curious quality of voting behavior that for large numbers of people motivation is weak if not almost absent. It is assumed that this motivation would gain its strength from the citizen's perception of the difference that alternative decisions made to him. Now when a person buys something . . . there are direct and immediate consequences for him. But for the bulk of the American people the voting decision is not followed by any direct, immediate, visible personal consequences . . . The ballot is cast, and for most people that is the end of it. If their side is defeated, it doesn't really matter.[5]

Curiously, this general lack of involvement means that the final vote decision is the consequence of *any* or *all* of a whole series of pressures relating to party loyalty, social and family characteristics, exposure to communications, perceived saliency of issues, and expectations as to who will win the election. All these variables, while vital to long-term understanding, create short-term measurement and conceptual problems that actually impede the task of predicting short-term fluctuations. The voting researcher, in common with the marketing researcher, invariably resolves this dilemma by choosing to measure partisan attitudes, in the hope of maximizing predictive power while dealing with a minimum number of variables.

According to Campbell *et al.* (1960, page 33) the predictive power of partisan attitudes is a consequence of (1) minimizing the effect of intervening variables, (2) restricting measurement to relevent conditions that are already personal, and (3) observing events after they have received their political translation, so that

---

5. Berelson, Lazarsfeld, and McPhee (1954, page 308).

4

the conditions of uncertainty that surround prediction of the voter's interpretation (or awareness) of events are excluded from the system.

In marketing, as we implied earlier, there has been some concern over the predictive power of attitudes, but few serious empirical attempts to find out how well they predicted. But in voting there has been a strong empirical tradition designed, in part, to test the usefulness of attitudes. It has lead to the development of the panel technique (Lipset *et al.*, 1954; and Lazarsfeld *et al.*, 1944) which in itself has contributed much to marketing analysis. Equally important, the findings on the influences on the predictive ability of attitudes are highly relevant to this present endeavor.

The best work on this problem has been done by a group at the University of Michigan Survey Research Center (Stokes *et al.*, 1958; and Campbell *et al.*, 1960). Their hypothesis was that, "the voting act depends in an immediate sense on the individual voter's evaluative orientations toward *several* objects of politics."[6] Six dimensions were identified for study during the 1952 and 1956 Presidential elections: the personal attributes of each candidate, the two political parties, the comparative record of the two parties, and the issue of domestics and foreign policy. Each respondent was located on each of these dimensions according to the direction and intensity of partisan attitude. Although the results are impressive

Table I–I—Predictive Power of Partisan Attitudes[a]

When Prediction Is from:	Correlation of Predictors with Voting Choice[b]	Proportion Correctly Classified
Attitude toward Eisenhower only	0.52	75%
Attitude toward Eisenhower and attitude on domestic issues	0.59	79%
All six dimensions of partisan attitude	0.71	86%

a Campbell *et al.* 1960, page 74.
b Using the point biserial correlation to measure the relationship between attitude toward Eisenhower and voting choice, and multiple regression for the relation between the voting act and the six dimensions of partisan attitudes.

6. In a marketing context this hypothesis would read "the brand choice act depends in an immediate sense on the individual buyer's evaluative orientations toward several attributes of the brand."

5

we should keep in mind that the goal was to predict a dichotomous choice where even a guess has a 0.5 (approximate) probability of being right. For this reason alone we cannot expect to do so well in predicting brand choice behavior when there are many brands that can be chosen.

Table 1–1 shows the power of one, two, and six dimensions of attitude in predicting the choice of Eisenhower for president in 1956. The contribution of the single scale evaluating Eisenhower is high when one considers that a presidential vote is much more than a choice of a man based on personal preference, it includes the choice of a farm policy, a foreign policy, and so forth. Also, despite the self-fulfilling aspect of voting intentions, the proportion of voters correctly predicted by partisan attitudes was higher than the proportion of voters who could predict their own behavior correctly.

Surprisingly, both parties received the largest portion of their votes from the moderate or neutral categories (see Table 1–2). Perhaps the most interesting feature of Table 1–2, vis-à-vis the analysis strategy followed in this report, is the consideration of the deviant cases. The question was, "What factors can explain the partisan choices of those for whom we were in error, particularly when behavior seems strongly to have contradicted the direction of partisan attitude?" Inspection of the interview protocols for the deviant cases suggested that false reporting of behavior and attitude change, induced by events after the pre-election interview, was only of moderate significance. This conclusion is strongly supported by several later studies directed at finding whether or not

Table I-2—Relation of Single Partisan Attitude to Division of Vote[a]

(Attitude Toward Eisenhower)

	UNFAVORABLE					FAVORABLE			
	-3	-2	-1	0	$+1$	$+2$	$+3$	$+4$	$+5$
Percent voting									
Republican	6	19	21	44	69	79	86	94	98
Number of cases	35	73	151	275	232	216	139	99	46

a Campbell et al., 1960.

6

the outcome of the 1964 Presidential election in California was influenced by the early reporting of returns from the east coast (Mendelsohn, 1965; and Lang and Lang, 1965). Further error was attributed to equal weights being assigned to each attitude dimension, where it was later apparent that one dimension was of overriding importance. And for some people, additional forces, such as the perceived preferences of primary group associates, had the greatest bearing on the decision. Usually these additional forces were absorbed into the preference structure, but cases were found, "where the wife voted her husband's preference either against her own inclination or without developing perceptions of her political environment" (Campbell *et al.*, 1960).

The major source of error, in predicting partisan choice, was uncovered when the sample was divided according to reported time of vote decision. Correlation (R) of partisan attitude with partisan choice ranged from 0.80 for the group who knew all along how they would vote, down to 0.25 for the group who decided less than two weeks before election day. Further analysis of the "deviants" showed that most of this group were subject to cross-pressures or attitude conflict. In the voting sense this has been defined (Berelson *et al.*, 1954, page 284) as "combinations of characteristics which, in a given context, would tend to lead the individual to vote on both sides of a contest". This group has its analogue in the category of buyers that make a brand choice when they can't distinguish clearly between competing brands—or possibly, just aren't interested in brand differences even if they do exist. However as buying experience accumulates, or the pressures of the campaign increase as election day comes closer, Berelson *et al.* (1954) have found that there is an increasing tendency toward consistency in all relevant aspects. This conclusion has been well supported in the literature on attitude change where the various mechanisms of achieving consistency—or in the brand choice context, of becoming convinced that there are meaningful differences between brands—have been extensively explored.

Consumer Attitudes and Durable Goods Expenditures

When Keynes (1935) formulated the consumption function, as the central element of his attack on the classical axioms of investment, he triggered the economists' deep and enduring interest in forecasting gross expenditures. Much of the attention has been directed at the most volatile element, which is consumer durables. Early attempts at specifying a relationship between income (changes) and expenditure level (changes) were largely unsatisfactory, because the consumer was not accorded autonomy in the timing and amount of his expenditures on durable goods.

Among the many critics of this artificial limitation[7] George Katona (1951 and 1960, for example) was the first to direct a major empirical effort, based on the hypothesis that consumers are subject to waves of pessimism and optimism that modify their response to purely financial variables such as changes in personal income. Unfortunately, the relevance of this long-term approach to the relationship of attitudes and economic behavior has been reduced by sharp differences of opinion on methodology and interpretation among researchers. However, a review of the basic points of view will at least indicate some of the problems that will have to be overcome in this present study.

Essentially Katona (and his co-worker Eva Mueller) believe that attitudes toward the economy, the price level, the families' expected financial situation, and an evaluation of buying conditions for durable goods have predictive value because "[an overall index] consistently foreshadowed fluctuations in discretionary spending in the six to nine months following the survey." For support they offer time series results such as the following, based on 22 consecutive quarterly surveys, for the population as a whole:

I. $\quad D = 0.18\,Y - 9.29 \qquad\qquad (r^2 = 0.50)$

II. $\quad D = 0.20\,Y + 0.31\,A - 43.34 \quad (R^2 = 0.80)$

Equation I is the relationship of consumer durables expenditures

---

7. See Duesenberry (1952) and Burns (1954).

(D) and disposable income (Y) in the six months following the survey. Equation II, and the associated coefficient of determination, shows the effect of the Survey Research Center Index (A) of Consumer Attitudes (Mueller, 1963). One surprising feature of this study, and a similar one by Adams (1964), is that the addition of specific buying intentions to the above equations does not improve the correlation. Mueller (1955) has explained this by pointing out that many consumers have short planning periods, the timing of their plans is uncertain, and plans can be changed easily. Furthermore, "it is the marginal buyer—who is hesitant and can wait— that accounts for a large part of the fluctuations in durable goods sales. Here intentions are least successful" (Mueller 1963).

Yet, using a different criteria of predictive value, Tobin (1959) came to exactly the opposite conclusion from the above. His conclusion was based on an analysis of a reinterview panel which showed that intentions were more closely related than attitudes to what people subsequently did. He raised a very difficult question, ". . . [can] one have confidence in the aggregative predictions based on overall proportions of favorable attitudes in a sample, if these attitudes bear no relation to the behavior of the individual who expressed them." The same question is often asked in marketing. So far the answer has usually been yes by default, for the kind of data that Tobin used are usually not available.

The only comparative study of aggregative time series and individual reinterview predictions using consumer attitudes has been reported by Adams (1965). His explanation of the paradox that a good predictor of aggregate consumer expenditures on durables can lack confirmation in reinterview (micro-economic) data is (1) that some individual relationship is definitely present, but is obscured by "inadequate measurement, failure to distinguish long-term effects or inter-personal differences from short-term movements, or selection of the wrong predictive time horizon," but (2) that a good deal of the strong aggregate relationship is a consequence of serial correlation as well as the over-time movement of other cyclical variables with which attitudes are correlated. The nature of these "other" variables is entirely con-

9

jectural, but evidently has to do with a community state-of-mind. In these circumstances measures of intentions or buying plans become attractive alternatives.

The strongest proponent, and keenest student, of intentions as predictors of purchase behavior is Thomas Juster (particularly 1964). Some of his work parallels Tobin's in the emphasis on reinterview studies. In one interesting study he fitted linear and non-linear functions to the relationship of attitude—then, of intentions—to the subsequent number of purchases. First, he did not find significantly non-linear results. Second, his r^2 for the attitude index were of the order of 0.01 while R^2 for two measures of intentions considered simultaneously ranged from 0.10 to 0.20.

In contrast with the results obtained in the voting studies cited above, these results are quite dismal. About all they imply is that intenders will purchase at a somewhat higher rate than non-intenders. In fact, in Juster's most recent summary of the value of intentions he stated, "Right now we don't know why the fulfilment rate is so poor or why the bulk of actual purchases is accounted for by non-intenders" (Juster 1966). His strategy for the time being is to improve his measures by using an explicit scale of purchase probability, rather than gross categories of "definitely, probably, no" or "don't know." His hope is that there is not too much deviation between prospects and behavior.

Insights from Within a Marketing Context

Virtually every marketing study that has looked at brand attitudes and brand choice behavior together has concluded that a relationship exists. Now, from the review of related efforts in voting and economic forecasting we have seen that such a general statement raises several basic questions. First, what criteria are being used to demonstrate the predictive value[8] of attitudes? That

8. By using predictive "value," rather than "validity," as the criteria I hope to avoid some of the premature rigor regarding causal factors and truth in an absolute sense that validity implies. Predictive value also seems more appropriate in this

is, are aggregate or individual comparisons being made, and are they based on data from only one point in time or over a period of time? Second, how strong is the relationship and what is the functional form? And third, what are the important influences on the predictive relationship and what is the nature of their influence? Only when this last question has been addressed can we begin to gain real understanding about the relationship.

A sampling of marketing studies will be discussed below according to the criteria of predictive value that was used. The sampling does not reflect the fact that many marketing studies use the aggregate and concurrent criteria where all the data are collected from a single cross-section survey.[9] These are generally unpublished, proprietary studies designed to answer specific operating questions.

To the extent that all of the studies to be examined are confined to specific operating problems we cannot expect them directly to pursue an understanding of the relationship (as would be demanded by the three questions posed earlier). Yet one becomes uneasy when re-reading Tobin's incisive question (cited above) to think that this kind of data must be relied on to advance our understanding. Greater cause for uneasiness will be introduced when we turn, from the state of empirical knowledge, to the pressures from within marketing for greater understanding.

Criterion I: Concurrent Measures of Brand Attitudes and Brand Usage

A typical example of an aggregate analysis using concurrent measures is an early study by Brown (1950). The same basic approach can be found in most cross-sectional surveys that audit test markets or ongoing national markets for periodic shifts in brand usage and preference. Brown used the method of successive intervals to have the respondent scale brands on a five-point scale

---

situation where we are dealing with a set of variables that have strong operational meaning.

9. The *aggregate* proportions of the total sample that like the brand and that use the brand are known, but the number of *individuals* that like and use the brand at the same time are not reported.

according to how satisfactory they were (from very satisfactory to very unsatisfactory). His usage data were based simply on whether or not the respondent was using the brand. The results are provocative, but much more information is necessary to make sense out of them. For example, see his findings in two of the five product markets presented in Table 1–3.

From the data in this table one can only infer that lack of preference is usually associated with low usage. A relatively simple extension of the analysis, to relate individual attitudes and usage, would give some idea of the strength of this inference, as well as insights into conditions of strong preference and low usage and vice versa. Even if this were done, the attitude scales are so poorly constructed as to eliminate any possibility of discriminating among brands—or among people. Clearly, if attitudes are to relate even to concurrent behavior the scales must be sensitive enough for brands that are perceived as different to be rated as different.

Despite the impediments to understanding inherent in linking gross proportions of the population holding a certain intensity of brand attitude to the proportion using the brand *at the same time*, it is used with surprising frequency. For example, Banks (1961) used multiple regression analysis to relate share of last purchase to measures of price, preference, and distribution and advertising

Table I-3—Attitudes Toward Brands and Market Usage[a]
(Selected product classes—Chicago 1949)

Product Class	Brand	Percent of Housewives Who Know Brand	Percent of Product Users Who Give Brand Top Rating	Percent of Housewives Now Using Brand
Scouring Cleanser	A	95.1%	45.7%	41.2%
	B	62.8	44.9	16.3
	C	43.6	29.4	11.0
	D	36.0	46.7	10.0
	E	65.8	24.6	6.1
Packaged Pie Mix	A	70.8%	24.3%	11.3%
	B	55.2	26.8	6.1
	C	51.0	44.2	10.9
	D	46.2	20.8	4.2
	E	23.3	24.2	3.3

a Brown, 1950.

12

expenditure.[10] The brand preference measure had a clear and marked effect in explaining coffee brand shares, but was quite subordinate in the cleanser market. Ehrenberg (1966) has elevated the relation of the percentage of people intending to buy a brand (I) and the current usership level (U), into a quasi-law expressed as:

$$I = K\sqrt{U} \pm 3\%$$

Apparently this relationship holds for large and small brands in over 30 different food, soap, and related product fields. The shape of the relationship is determined by the additional knowledge: "(a) that current users of a brand virtually all say that they intend to buy it again, and (b) that for current non-users such an intention varies with the recency or the frequency of their past usage (if any) of the brand." Two systematic deviations were noted, although both were within the limits of fit of $\pm 3\%$. First, fewer than predicted from the current usership level say they intend to buy a successful new brand. And conversely, more than predicted by current usership say they will buy a dying brand. This is explained as reflecting differences in the number of past users relative to current users because some past users usually express an intent-to-buy in addition to the current users. At a more general level, to be followed in this report, this implies an environment where increasing numbers are encouraged to buy a new brand or, conversely, deterred from buying an old, dying brand.

---

10. The following are the regression coefficients reported by Banks (1961) for two separate products (the independent variable being each brand's share of the last purchase of the product). The high R^2 for cleansers may be due to the loss of degrees of freedom.

	Cleanser (9 Brands) $R^2 = .999$	Coffee (21 Brands) $R^2 = .792$
Brand Preference	.368	1.108
Average Price	−.436	−.202
Store Coverage	.150	.609
Store Display	.224	−.364
Promotional Effort	.416	.067
POP Advertising	−.242	−.207
Advertising Expenditure	.143	−.536

13

One plausible implication of Ehrenberg's finding is that for markets without a major short-term trend of any kind, there is a stable relationship between brand attitudes (or one component of them at any rate) and concurrent reports of brand usage. As such, attitudes in this context should have predictive value—at least at the *aggregate* level. This simple implication is unfortunately made suspect by a study by Appel (1966). To anticipate slightly, it was shown that there was a strong attitude–behavior relationship at the individual level which had to be taken into account before an aggregate relationship could be found.

The study design began with the selection of eight groups of three matched markets. Then one member of each group was randomly assigned to a control (no advertising) condition, while the other two received different, although dollar-equivalent, advertising plans. The purpose was to measure the effect of the two advertising plans, relative to the effect of no advertising at all, according to the criteria of (1) single brand unaided recall awareness, (2) brand attitude measured by paired comparisons, and (3) brand usage in the past two weeks. The results, as summarized in Table 1–4, were determined by taking the percentage difference between the mean value of the criterion variable, in each of the two advertised markets and the control market, and summing across the eight groups.

The results are perplexing until it is realized that (1) the test was of very short duration (apparently two weeks), (2) in a long-established market with a brand that had enjoyed almost 100 per cent trial, (3) the advertising was very similar in appeal and format to that which had been used for years, and (4) paired comparisons

Table 1-4—Effects of Advertising upon Brand Awareness, Usage, and Attitude[a]

$\sum_{1}^{8}$ Markets	Plan A Minus Control Mean	Plan B Minus Control Mean
Brand awareness	+0.4%	+1.8%
Brand attitude	−0.4%	+1.0%
Brand usage	+4.3%	+6.1%

a Appel, 1966, pages 141–152.

14

are the worse possible measure of subtle changes in attitude (see for example Greenberg, 1963; and Blankenship, 1966). The wonder is that any change, particularly in usage, was observed. An examination of the link between individual attitude and usage uncovers the reason for the jump in usage seen in Table 1–4. Appel calls this the moderating effect of attitudes (see Table 1–5). Moderating "effect" may be a useful way of looking at the influence of attitudes in this case. Obviously the advertising created no incentive for the non-user, or very limited user, groups to change their feelings and behavior. But it did an effective job of either reinforcing the attitudes of those already predisposed, or merely reminding them to stock up. A follow-up study, several weeks after the conclusion of the advertising test, would be required to separate these two hypotheses.

Most concurrent measurement of attitudes and behavior is done for descriptive purposes. That is, it is used to answer such specific one–time questions as: Has the trend in favorableness of evaluation of cereal brands A, B, and C among heavy users of cereal gone up in the last year? Generally such narrowly focused attitude research does little to confer understanding.

The major exception to this conclusion is found in a series of studies reported by Achenbaum (1966a and b). The overall approach is based on concurrent measurements, but is designed to uncover the specific attitude components most useful in understanding the overall evaluation. Because it is the most advanced "system" to be found in this measurement category, and provides some useful generalizations, it merits close attention.

Table I-5—Brand Attitude as a Moderator of Advertising Effectiveness[a]

(Percent of respondents reporting usage)

	Least Favorable Attitude	More Favorable Attitude	Most Favorable Attitude
Control Market	10.1%	32.5%	45.7%
Plan A/Plan B Markets (Average)	11.3	38.1	53.5
Improvement—Absolute	+1.2	+5.6	+7.8

a Appel, 1966.

Achenbaum first establishes, to his satisfaction at any rate, that his approach is predictive because he has observed a very direct relationship between reports of overall evaluation and recent usage given at the same time. See, for example, Table 1–6.

The next step is to have a group of prospects, for the product class being studied, rate the desirability of the *product* having 40 to 130 different attributes and benefits. The purpose of this step is to uncover the factors involved in the consumer's evaluation of the product, according to their generic importance. Factor analysis permits the reduction of the basic list of phrases into ten or so logical groups, or dimensions, which can be identified according to the basic benefit or attribute they tap.

Following this, one or two items or phrases are selected (by their factor loading) which best represent each dimension. A large cross-section sample is asked to rate the key competitive *brands* on these items plus an overall evaluative scale. A regression analysis using competitive comparisons as the input then identifies the item which is most highly correlated with the overall comparative brand rating. This is presumably the attribute or benefit with the greatest competitive leverage, which should then receive promotional emphasis (assuming the brand can support any claim on the benefit or attribute). It is interesting to note that the evaluation of the brand on a specific feature is never more closely related to usage than the overall evaluation. Logically, of course, the overall scale should subsume all the other relevant items.

SOME METHODOLOGICAL PROBLEMS

The approach taken by Achenbaum has undeniable diagnostic

Table 1-6—Relationship Between Concurrent Attitudes and Usage for Selected Brands of Consumer Products[a]

	(ACCORDING TO PERCENT USING)			
Brand Rating	Cigarette Brand	Deodorant Brand	Gasoline Brand	Laxative Brand
Excellent	68%	44%	57%	65%
Very Good	23	30	36	27
Good	7	24	11	14
Fair to Poor	2	2	8	3

a Achenbaum, 1966a, page 113.

16

value. It can also be used to make generalizations about inter-product differences that provide many insights into buying behavior. Yet there are limitations, of unknown degree, inherent in the use of concurrent measures of usage behavior to demonstrate the value of attitudes.

First of all, it is past usage behavior that is being measured. In a *stable* market this might be related to future behavior with some accuracy if we were not dealing with the vagaries of memory decay, selective recall of information, and defensive forgetting (the relevant literature is fully described in Granbois and Engel, 1965). When a respondent cannot recall the sequence of recent purchases of a relatively unimportant household product she could follow several strategies; for example, guessing in such a way that her behavior is consistent with her attitudes if they have been elicited earlier in the interview, or responding with what she thinks should be the most popular brand. It is also possible in some product categories, such as cosmetics, for the most socially desirable response to be given. In the face of these problems most researchers limit themselves to asking about most recent usage of the product and which brands are usually bought.

All of the problems of recall measures were encountered by Parfitt (1967) in a study which interviewed members of a panel to obtain product and brand usage claims which could be compared to purchase data recorded by the diary panel. The respondents were not aware that the interview and the panel were connected in any way. The overall conclusion was that, "With notable exceptions, any attempt to recall behavior beyond the recent past (e.g., over the last month or the last three months etc.) tends to produce exaggeration or over-simplification which seriously distorts actual purchasing behavior." Inflation of usage claims ranged from 14 per cent for tea to 91 per cent for dentifrice. Statements about usual brand usage were found to be accurate for loyal and heavy buyers, but badly distorted overall by the large proportion who were infrequent or nonbuyers of the product and also claimed a usual brand. Parfitt's findings about inter-product differences in extent of error are similar but more extreme than those of Kirsch,

Berger, and Belford (1962). Their study used pantry checks instead of panel data to confirm telephone interview reports of "brand bought last." The advantage of this approach is the opportunity to identify some of the causes for error. In nine product classes there was 87 to 95 per cent agreement between the two measures. The greatest disparity was for toothpaste, apparently because the housewife is unaware or forgets that other members of the household have bought their own supply.

Leaving aside problems of accuracy, and the uncertainties of relating past behavior to future behavior in dynamic markets, the greatest shortcoming of a single report of recent usage is that it provides no useful information about loyalty patterns or the proportion of purchase volume devoted to the brand. Graustein (1966) emphasizes that discriminating among loyal and "in and out transients" is of greater importance than merely predicting the relative likelihood of purchasing a given brand.

In a few instances attitudes have been linked directly to adjacent aggregate market behavior. This is another approach to determining the predictive value of attitudes.

Criterion 2: Aggregate Brand Attitudes and
Adjacent Market Behavior

The crucial limitations of the concurrent criterion of predictive value is that all the data comes from one method at one point in time. A more demanding approach is to compare results between two methods at different times (Ray 1968). When talking about aggregate behavior this means a survey measure of attitudes and store audit or diary panel measures of market share.

The appropriate design is well illustrated by the Continuous Advertising Planning Program (CAPP) established by the Leo Burnett Company (Maloney, 1967). This is a multi-product study of changes in brand attitudes as measured by monthly mail surveys of independently drawn samples. The primary functions of CAPP are (1) to provide diagnostic information about the strengths and weaknesses of brands that can be used to establish advertising goals, (2) to evaluate advertising campaigns in terms of the goals, and (3) to identify areas where campaigns need improvement.

Two of the findings from this project are of particular relevance here. The first is the extremely high correlation between brand attitudes (as measured by the proportion of users who are satisfied with the brand) and Nielson market shares in the same time period. In no case was the correlation less than 0.9 across 25 brands in several product classes. Of greater interest here is the "tremendous multiplier effect [of point-of-purchase factors] upon the way in which shoppers respond to their readiness-to-buy inclinations" (Maloney, 1967, page 22). For example, the proportion buying a particular brand on sale or with a "special offer" varied, from 19 per cent among those who preferred the brand, to 28 per cent of those who thought it was as good as one or more brands, to 43 per cent among those who didn't think it was one of the better brands. In other words, point-of-purchase factors have the greatest facilitating effect on those who are least favorable toward the brand.

Despite the strong relationship between aggregate attitudes and market share at the same point in time, it is not at all clear that *changes* in attitude will predict *changes* in behavior in a time series sense. An indication of what might happen is reported by Haskins (1964). In this study a number of experimental markets were exposed to 50 per cent more advertising than the normal control markets for a period of nine months. Attitudes, knowledge levels, and actual sales were measured each month for a new brand and an old brand. The net effect of the advertising (test minus control condition) was a slow and persistent rise in sales for the new brand and a relatively rapid rise and rapid decline in sales for the established product. Both these sales curves were paralleled by the attitude curves when allowance was made for a time lag between attitudes and sales. The knowledge curve, however, was unrelated to either sales curve.

Studies of trend relationships between aggregate attitudes and behavior are difficult to appraise in the form they are presented by Haskins and Maloney, because of an awkward data artifact. The problem arises because the interval between attitude change and purchase is usually shorter than the interval between independent surveys (as in the CAPP design) or between the before and after phases of the typical study of communication effects. This means, for example, that "An advertiser who regularly obtains both attitude and sales measures will, if his advertising is communicating, see the effects in sales increases *before* they show up as communication changes" (Ramond, 1965, page 151). The mistaken inference would be that attitude change follows change in market share. There are, of course, reasons why this might actually happen at the individual level. Because of post-decision dissonance a recent buyer may change his attitude, after experience with the brand, in order to justify the choice (Ehrlich, 1957).

The extent to which aggregate attitude change either leads or follows change in market share has been studied by Day and Assael (1968). A number of direct effect and distributed lag time series models (see Palda, 1964) were fitted to bi-monthly data extending over four years. The results for 13 brands consistently showed that attitudes have a strong leading effect. The only circumstances in which attitude change followed market share change to any degree were those in which there was a consistent trend in the market share. Another consistent finding was a pronounced lag between the attitude change and the market share change. As long as this was taken into account satisfactory predictions of market share change were obtained.

The three studies reviewed above largely cover the published research using this aggregate criterion, with the exception of several studies that deal primarily with product preferences (Harris, 1964; Crespi, 1964;[11] USDA, 1956; Banks, 1950). Some insights into the relationship of attitudes and behavior have been gained, but on balance the aggregation concealed more than it revealed.

---

11. For example Crespi found that the gross rentals of movies can be predicted when attitude data such as audience enjoyment and interest in seeing the picture are combined with other measures such as advertising penetration.

*Criterion 3: Individual, Over-Time Comparisons of
Attitudes and Brand Choice Behavior*

At the outset it was stated that this report was directed toward understanding "the predictive relationship of brand attitudes with subsequent brand choice behavior . . . (and) the influences that operate, between the expression of the attitude and the purchase decisions, to modify the effect of the attitude". In studies of voting behavior and the forecasting value of intentions having the same goals, panel designs were utilized to achieve these goals. Now we turn to the use of this design in the study of brand attitudes for specific guidance on the kinds of relationships and influences that should be considered.

The studies discussed below appear to exhaust the published literature on panel measures of attitude and brand choice behavior. The coverage is, if anything, broader within this particular problem area than are recent surveys of marketing applications of panel methodology by Nicosia (1965), Granbois and Engel (1965), and Palda (1965). Nicosia concluded that cost was a possible, but not a compelling reason for the generally limited use of panels. The virtually exclusive use of time-series and trend data and analysis, in situations where panel designs were clearly more appropriate, was ascribed to a "cultural lag" traceable to historical reliance on the theory and methods of economics. Wider future use of panel designs and analysis was thought to hinge on acceptance of the need to observe the same individuals in order to understand the influences on predictions and disclose the direction of causation under conditions of change.

The oldest, and still the most immediately useful, of the studies to be reviewed here was reported by Banks (1950–51). The data of interest here are from a panel of 465 households in the city of Chicago. There was an initial interview to collect (1) preferences for brands in seven grocery product categories on an eight-point asymmetrical rating scale using "satisfactory" as the basic word in the descriptions, (2) intentions-to-buy brands in each product category, and (3) classification information. Following this the

21

panel members kept weekly mail diaries of their purchases—but only for a three-week period. The members were interviewed again at the end of the panel for additional preference data on two products, and asked why there was a discrepancy (if any) between stated intentions, preferences, and purchases of two products (scouring cleanser and coffee).

The most interesting feature is the large disparity between the effectiveness of aggregate versus individual predictions of purchase. The simple correlation between aggregate preference (absolute number of extremely favorable ratings for each brand) and the brand's share of the actual purchases of the product class ranged from 0.670 for coffee to 0.985 for peanut butter.[12] The weighted mean correlation for the seven products was 0.918. At the individual level only intentions were used to predict individual brand choice, apparently because of the close relation between intentions and high preference ratings. Of those who said they intended to buy some brand(s), 61.8 per cent carried out their intention fully, 19.1 per cent carried out their intention partially, and 19.6 per cent switched completely. There is no way of knowing just how much of this performance represents a "self-fulfilled prophecy," that is, purchases made to satisfy a previously expressed intention. But this factor cannot be ignored because of the very short duration of the panel. On the other hand there is a plausible variability within product classes, that is, with an impulse item like ice cream only 39 per cent of the brand intentions were fulfilled.

The short duration of the panel did provide an opportunity to ask the members directly their reasons for not fulfilling their brand intentions. Even after recognizing that the responses may be rationalizations made in order to look good, or guesses because the real reason could not be recalled, this approach does have exploratory value. The most frequently stated reason for switching to another brand of coffee was lack of availability, followed in

---

12. The correlations between intentions and share of recent purchases, using the brand's share of the panel inventory at the time of the first interview, were 0.986 and 0.977 respectively.

order by desire for a change and price reductions on other brands. The ordering of reasons for scouring cleansers was exactly reversed, indicating that interbrand differences are not as salient in cleansers as in coffee. No quantitative analysis of the impact of these three variables was given. However, even this limited, qualitative attempt to determine why attitudes (or one component at any rate) do not predict is unusual.

The purchase decision process for durable goods lends itself to longitudinal analysis. The decision itself is usually characterized by considerable prior planning and a long repurchase cycle, so that it is important for the manufacturer to separate the immediate from the long-term effects of his marketing program.

A good example of the analytical value of panel data is provided by Pratt (1965). Intentions toward purchases of appliances, as well as the expected brand, were collected from 6000 households during personal interviews. A reinterview, a year later, showed that only 37 per cent of these intentions were fulfilled. The fulfilment rate varied widely by product type, brand, and the level of commitment to the intention (see Table 1–7).

This table suggests that the expectations of Brand A intenders are being supported by additional knowledge and the ongoing marketing activities of Brand A (encountered between the interview and the purchase), while the expectations of Brand B intenders are not. This inference was further supported when an *aggregate* index of initial attitude toward each brand made no appreciable contribution to an understanding of the differential fulfilment rates. Pratt argues that this means current promotional efforts are

Table I-7—Comparison of Appliance Buying Intentions and Behavior[a]

(For three national brands)

Brand	Proportion of Intenders Actually Buying the Appliance as Planned	Percent of Buyers Who Purchased Brand as Intended
A	44%	68%
B	42%	24%
C	30%	57%

a Pratt, 1965, page 249.

23

relatively more important than predispositions, "in terms of impact on purchase decisions for durable goods, particularly the impact on decisions of intenders who change their minds about brand." However this conclusion is debatable until it is tested using attitudes, at the individual level, as predictors of the purchases of intenders and non-intenders together.[13]

The ambitious General Motors advertising effectiveness research program (Smith, 1965) uses a hybrid of intentions and evaluative components as a measure of preference. They find that each level of preference has its own economic value according to its associated probability of subsequent purchase and dealer visitation (measured by a two re-interviews at six month intervals). Table 1–8 indicates what would have happened to sales of a disguised General Motors car, the "Watusi," if all the people in the sample[14] had purchased a car within three months of the initial interview.

Once the economic value of each preference level has been established, the levels are treated as market segments. Media plans are drawn up that will focus on a specific preference level, in order

Table 1-8—Value of Preference Levels in Terms of Probability of Purchase and Dealer Visitation[a]

	Preference Level (Percent) March 1965	Probability Will Visit "Watusi" Dealer	Probability Will Buy "Watusi"
"Watusi" first choice	5%	.840	.560
"Watusi" in consideration class	7	.620	.220
"Watusi" in buying class	8	.400	.090
Aware of "Watusi"	14	.240	.050
Not aware of "Watusi"	66	.015	.004
	100%		

a Smith, 1965.

13. Haskins (1964) has some evidence from an unpublished study of over–time changes in a measure related to intentions, showing that shifts in attitudes toward brands are much less pronounced than corresponding shifts in intentions.

14. Smith (1965) presents data only for a sample of male heads of households in which the family car was purchased new. There is no indication as to how exhaustive this sub-sample is of the entire sample. Also the data are estimated from a selective reinterview plan in which only a small proportion of those who "definitely will not buy any car" are contacted again.

to move it up a notch. The related copy objectives are drawn up by referring to differences in brand ratings on specific attributes between preference levels. For example, if the "buying class" and "consideration class" groups vary substantially in rating only one attribute, such as trade-in value, changing this attitude becomes one of the copy objectives. Finally, reach and frequency goals are tailored to the worth of moving people up a preference level.

Most of the analysis reported by Smith appears to have been done on a semi-aggregative basis, that is, assuming homogeneity within preference levels. This is reasonably defensible as a first approximation. However, analysis at the individual level with respect to "lost" sales, contrasting non-buyers and buyers from the first choice class, and also of sales gained from other preference levels, is necessary to understand the nature of the brand attitude–brand choice relationship and pick out shortcomings in the current promotional efforts. If we know why they didn't buy this time perhaps steps can be taken to prevent future losses of sales.

Several other studies will be mentioned because they illuminate the brand attitude–brand choice relationship, although this was not the main concern: (A) Abrams (1966) was interested in comparing several rating scales according to their sensitivity and predictability. Specifically, "it is predicted that the brand rated highest, or tied for highest will be the brand on hand," (that is, on the household's shelf in a follow-up pantry survey, three months after the brands were rated). Although the measures of attitude and behavior were very gross, and the interbrand differences slight, only 10 per cent of the predictions were incorrect. For another 22 per cent the brand on hand was tied in rating with one of the other brands. (B) Another study, reported by Rothman (1964), was also interested in the predictive value of several ingenious attitude measures. However, the behavior measure was not subsequent purchase, but response to an offer to subsidize the purchase of the rated brands. Even with this odd and seemingly biased response measure the results were as expected. (C) By far the most complete study of the comparative value of attitude measures is reported by Axelrod (1968). The method was to apply the three criteria of

(1) ability to discriminate between advertising treatments, (2) reliability, and (3) predictive power, to ten different measures. Two of the measures, first brand awareness and a constant sum scale, were able to satisfy all criteria. Of particular interest is the finding that long–run (five months) switching and repeat buying behavior could be predicted just as well as short-run (five weeks) behavior. Two important limitations were that only premium (non-price) brands were included, and the behavior measure was last-time usage.[15] Had these limitations been relaxed it is probable that random and other influences would have had a much greater effect on the long-run predictions. (D) Brown presents some interesting data as the result of a panel study of the influences of various family members on the make of auto purchased (see Table 1–9). Two points are worth noting. First, that the strong relationship of preference and purchase is strongly influenced by the fact that "60–70 per cent of automobile-buying families tend to repeat the make purchased, primarily as a result of their inability to predict with certainty the outcome of a decision to purchase any other given make of car."[16] Second, the primary reason for purchasing

Table 1–9—Influence of Family Members on Brand Choice (1956)[a]

Make Purchased Was Preferred by:	Number	Percent
Both Husband and Wife	296	42.1
Neither Husband nor Wife	246	35.0
Husband Only	99	14.1
Wife Only	62	8.8
Total Number of Purchases	703	100.0

a Brown, 1961, page 78.

15. The Advertising Research Foundation (1967 Annual Report) has mentioned plans to initiate several studies with goals very similar to those pursued by Axelrod. The major difference will be the use of a consumer diary panel to record purchase data.

16. This statement appears equally valid today in the light of the results of a study predicting new car ownership reported by Ito (1967). This study was unfortunately flawed by inadequate attitude scales. The scales used were generally unable to predict loyal and switching behavior of Ford and Chevrolet owners. Here the proportions who remained loyal included 72 per cent of Ford owners and 94 per cent of Chevrolet owners.

a make other than the one preferred, "was the discovery that the actual price was higher than the expected price." (E) The most disappointing, in terms of usefulness, is NBC's (1955) study of the changes in preference and buying behavior due to the advent of television. The data were collected during an interview just before a new television station went on the air, and a re-interview six months later. The data are sketchy and were only presented for the group who bought a TV set between the two surveys; not for a control (unexposed) group. For Scotties tissue, which was advertised on television, preference increased 24 (absolute) percentage points, while the number buying at least once in the previous month increased 20 percentage points. For Kleenex, which did not advertise on TV, preference declined 24 percentage points, while the number buying in the past month decreased by 8 percentage points. The main finding of relevance is the difference in degree of "elasticity" between attitude and behavior change.

The Problem of Attitude Change and Behavior Change

The orientation of this study, and of almost all the studies reviewed here, is toward the relationship of attitudes to subsequent behavior. A closely related question concerns the effect of a change in attitudes on subsequent behavior. Often these two problems merge together, as when groups are identified as having different attitudes, because they were differentially exposed to marketing stimuli, and the problem is to find out how the behavior of the groups differs (for instance, Appel, 1966). The question of changes over time is also, as we have seen, an issue in time series studies. However, both these approaches involve aggregations which conceal a great deal of activity at the individual level.

At the present time, surprisingly little is known about the individual behavioral consequences of a change in attitude. To some extent the lack of research activity represents an expression of faith that a relationship does exist; but it is more likely that the complexities of the reinterview panel design have been the main obstacle. Some idea of the appropriate design can be gathered

27

from the above description of the General Motors study, although the analysis was not concerned with change at the individual level. Recently two studies[17] were completed which incorporate the necessary three wave reinterview panel (Dubois, 1967; and Achenbaum, 1967).[18] Because the two studies are similar in intent and results we will focus on the implications of the Achenbaum results.

Three waves of telephone interviews with 4000 housewives were spaced at three month intervals. Aggregate attitudes (on a six point evaluative scale) and reported usage were found to be very stable for nineteen individual brands—seldom varying more than one percentage point between interviews. However, when these brands were combined and individual responses were studied, a great deal of individual activity was uncovered. Typically, in a three month period, a third of the original users became non-users, while eight per cent of non-users became users. Also, only 48 per cent of the brand ratings remained the same in both interviews. The two types of change were found to be very closely linked; for example an upward shift of one point on the rating scale between June and September almost doubled the probability that a non-user in September would become a user by December—that is, the probability increased from 11 to 19 per cent. These results were consistent across brands, and were similar with other kinds of scales. This constitutes strong evidence for a causal relationship, but with a strong qualification that only some behavior change appears associated with prior attitude change. No doubt different spacings of the panel interviews would give different results, and there is always the problem of distinguishing true change from response unreliability. Even with these considerations there appear to be a significant number of occasions when environmental influences

---

17. Several similar studies are in progress using data from the Columbia University Research Project on Buyer Behavior. In one study (Day, 1969) a continuous-time, discrete-state stochastic model is being used to evaluate the effect of changes in marketing stimuli, as well as actual behavior, on the rate of formation of attitudes toward new brands.

18. The forerunner to this study was Dubois (1960).

contribute to behavior change, yet are not reflected in behavior change.

Pressures for Greater Understanding

Our assumptions about the nature of the attitude–subsequent behavior relationship impinge on our understanding and reactions toward many significant marketing problems. Sometimes evidence concerning the predictive power of attitudes is of only peripheral interest. However, in the marketing problem (or opportunity) areas to be discussed below, a viable theoretical or practical approach depends to a considerable extent on this relationship. To be sure there are numerous other weak links in our understanding. But because attitudes are often chosen to represent the net effect of other variables, and are an essential feature of empirical testing or verification, further progress in these problem areas is often contingent upon an improved understanding of the functioning of attitudes.

The goal here is to outline briefly the place and importance of the attitude–behavior relationship in the particular marketing problem area. Nothing so ambitious as even a partial survey of the literature will be attempted.

The Changing Competitive Environment

It is easy to endow the market environment of the recent past with all the features of the present. Yet it was not too long ago that gross attitude and behavior measures were quite appropriate to isolate the simple and clear–cut physical differences between brands, products, or advertisements.

According to the historical perspective of Burns Roper (1966), we now have a situation where: "product differentiation has come close to disappearing. A related change is that the level of performance of most products today is far greater than what the

29

consumer needs. A third change is the sheer number of products, brands and packages consumers have to choose among today. A fourth characteristic of the state of technology today is the rate of product appearance and disappearance, and the rate of change and development among the products that stay around, which is nothing less than staggering." In this view it is inevitable that the focus of research should increasingly shift toward the measurement of the "subtleties and complexities of images and attitudes . . . and the most elusive question of all [which is] how are these attitudes reflected in action."

The Measurement of Advertising Effectiveness

This thorny problem has provided a continuing impetus to the study of the value of attitudes (or attitude change). Recently the impetus has become stronger, as the alternative measures of effectiveness such as sales effects, changes in awareness, and factual recall have proven invalid or more difficult to isolate (Haskins, 1964; and Achenbaum, 1964).

In some respects the use of attitudinal criteria is a bow to expediency. Attitudes show larger and more immediate effects than could ever be expected with purchase (sales) results. The research design is usually simple, inexpensive, can provide results immediately after the advertising under test has appeared and can be related to the results of post-tests of alternatives. Under the appropriate conditions attitude measures have very useful diagnostic properties.

The growing popularity of attitude measures has been accompanied by refinements in the long-held hypothesis of a "hierarchy of effects" (see Lavidge and Steiner, 1961; and the critical evaluation by Palda, 1966). This hypothesis essentially posits an increasing probability of purchase as an individual moves through the stages of awareness → knowledge → liking → preference → conviction. One of the more extreme but logically appealing implications of the "hierarchy," is that sales can be dispensed with as a criterion of effectiveness and intermediate variables used instead. This accounts for part of the influence of the widely used DAGMAR measurement procedure (Colley, 1961). Reliance on attitudes is also one of the strengths of the DAGMAR procedure, because it forces an explicit and specific statement of the objectives of the advertising in terms that are measurable with attitude variables (Smith, 1965).

As Palda has noted, there is now such general acceptance of the hierarchy of effects, that few are willing to conduct tests at more than one level at a time. This certainly helps to explain the paucity of studies linking attitude (change) and behavior (change). Yet the burden of the foregoing literature review was that the relationship is complex and non-obvious, even for the relatively simpler situation where there is no directed (or advertising induced) change of brand attitudes. The time is nearing when studies of advertising effectiveness will not be satisfied with an essentially simplistic view of the function of attitudes and will explicitly consider the influences on the attitude–behavior relationship. If Maloney is having his way, the time is undoubtedly already here:

We are finding that the gaps between laboratory tests and pretest occurrences, between pretest and survey phenomena, and between the survey and sales level are so filled with these "contaminating" influences [19] that they surely seem to be the major influences in the flow of advertising effects. We may have done more than we intended in tidying up our specialized, normalized, randomized and highly rationalized copy tests and effectiveness measures. In sweeping some of these factors under the rug, we meant to purify these measures, but we may have rendered them absolutely sterile! [20]

The Development of Theories of Buyer Behavior

A variety of theories and quasi-theories have been developed recently to explain various aspects of market behavior. Because many of them represent a synthesis of suggestive results from other

19. Maloney here is referring to variables which specifically "contaminate" the advertising evaluation process; such as the adequacy of the advertising weight, outside "noises" from competitive advertising or the advertiser's own packaging and display activity, and the timing of the exposures or expenditures (which go to make up the schedule of reinforcement).
20. Maloney (1963, page 94).

fields of study, their long-term usefulness in a marketing context depends on their ability to explain and relate various observable market phenomena, and ultimately to predict these phenomena.[21]

The most fully articulated theory at the buyer level has been presented by Howard and Sheth (1966 unpublished) and Howard (1963 and 1966). Their work has provided an impetus to this report, as well as guided some of the theoretical considerations. Within the theory, attitudes are given a central role as intervening variables which provide measurable inferences about a series of hypothetical constructs. The unmeasurable constructs, in turn, deal with the motives being satisfied by the purchase, the nature of the brands that will be perceived as purchase possibilities, and the decision rules which are used to structure the motives and alternatives in some fashion that is internally consistent. Because the decision rules are learned from past experience and selective exposure to current product and brand information, the structure of the constructs is constantly changing. A variety of other forces also influence this system, including the search for a satisfying equilibrium. The functioning of this dynamic system, and predictions about the effects of manipulations of the environment, can be inferred by attitude measures. However, they can also be inferred by measures of behavior—if appropriate consideration is given to situational variables which inhibit the choice of some brands in the set of all those being considered. The usefulness of the latter inferences clearly depends on detailed knowledge of these variables, which can only be gained by observing their influence on the attitude–subsequent behavior relationship.

The other comprehensive approach to understanding buyers is by Nicosia (1966). His main interest is in the sequence of events that lead to "consumer decision processes." By taking this approach he is able to develop a family of non-linear analytic models that yield many useful insights into brand choice behavior.

---

21. The pioneering theories of Lazarsfeld and Katona could also be included here; not only because they were comprehensive and incorporated attitudes as central elements, but also because they have many direct links with the two more recent theories described here. For a good review, see Glock and Nicosia (1963).

The elements to his over-time models include: "B—the final act . . . M—the consumer's motivation. A strong driving force . . . that specifically leads a consumer toward (a specific) brand . . . A— The consumer's attitude. A driving force that is weaker than M and not uniquely crystallized on brand X^{22} . . . C—The communication sent by a business firm." These variables are postulated to be linked in a series of simultaneous differential (with respect to time) equations. Some methods for estimating the parameters of the equations from panel data are discussed. The model predicts a wide variety of attitude–behavior relationships depending on various values of the parameters. If the parameters can be empirically estimated with acceptable accuracy then sensitive use of the models should do much to further our knowledge of the influence of attitudes and their role in buying behavior. However, the problems are many, as other less ambitious model builders have discovered.

The Need for Improved Functional Inputs to Models of Market Processes

The traditional approach has been to describe market processes *analytically* by first symbolizing the elements involved and then explicitly describing the functional forms connecting the elements. There are several crippling shortcomings to this approach (see Wells, 1963). First, the relevant market behavior must usually be described by highly aggregated market–wide variables. And second, a truly meaningful representation usually requires so many elements that it is virtually impossible to describe all the necessary inter-relationships. There is no guarantee that the alternative of *computer simulation* will perform any better. But at least with simulation there is the potential for describing each unit (buyer) as a separate entity, and then making them responsive to all the relevant variables for which data exists.

---

22. This definition of attitudes by Nicosia (1966, page 197) is quite different from that of most other users of the term. In fact a reversal of the definitions of motives and attitudes would seem to come closer to current practice in marketing and in the behavioral sciences.

The question of which approach is most fruitful will not be resolved until both are freed from the restrictions of inadequately stated functional relationships and excessive random error. And because attitudes are often used as proxies for other unmeasurable variables the attitude–behavior relationship is critical to the development of both groups of models:

1. *Analytical Models.* A non-stationary Markov process model, developed by Lipstein (1965) to relate advertising effort to purchase activity, appears to be particularly sensitive to the formulation of the attitude–behavior relationship. The model is built around a matrix (R) that represents the probability of consumer preference toward brands (1 to n) remaining fixed or shifting between two interviews within a certain time period. Lipstein unfortunately does not differentiate between basic response instability versus true change, and uses only the intentions component of attitude in a gross dichotomous form. Consequently the matrix is characterized by large entries in the diagonal. When R_0, the preference matrix in period zero, is different from R_1, the preference matrix in period one, Lipstein introduces a causative matrix (C) which is a measure of the effectiveness of the marketing innovation between periods:

$$R_0 C_0 = R_1$$

The C matrix can be related to advertising expenditures by brand to evaluate effectiveness of this innovation variable. By working backwards and relating the preference matrix (R) to a standard brand purchase switching matrix (A) the effect of advertising on sales can presumably be described. To make this relationship Lipstein argues that the A and R matrices differ only by the linear effect of availability of each Brand $j(d_j)$ and the price elasticity relative to other brands (p_j):

$$a_{ij} = [r_{ij} d_j (p_j + e_{ij})]$$

where a_{ij} and r_{ij} are components of the A and R matrices respectively and e_{ij} is an error component with expectation of zero. Although Lipstein uses an attitude matrix with built-in stability

34

and apparently gets useful results, there is no reason to expect that other more useful and more sensitive measures of attitude will conform to the linear relationship.

2. *Computer Simulation.* The most complex simulation undertaken in marketing to date has recently been completed by Amstutz (1966). It is based on "micro-analytic representations" of the buyer as well as retailer and distributor activities and the competitive interactions. One of the key response characteristics at the buyer level is the probability of seeking a particular brand[23] of product during a stated period. This probability function is based on a composite variable called the "perceived need for that brand." This composite variable increases with (1) positive attitude toward the brand,[24] as measured by an eleven point semantic differential scale, (2) the number of times the buyer *used* any brand in the product class during the preceding quarter, and (3) the time since the last purchase of any brand in the product class was made. Attempts to validate this particular relationship were not reviewed in the working paper cited here. Apparently, however, the results were acceptable, after adjustments were made for different effects within income groups. This kind of cutting and fitting does have some empirical interest, but one wonders just how stable and generalizable the net result will be in other time periods or for other product categories. The door is also left open for the inclusion of other variables—possibly leading to further obscuring of the basic relationship. In fairness, the simulator has more than enough to do, without investigating the basic characteristics of each of his response functions. But at present, as we have seen, he may not find too much assistance, at least not when it comes to the attitude–behavior relationship.

23. This particular relationship was chosen by Amstutz because of evidence that, "consumers entering a store with an explicit intention to investigate or acquire a particular brand exhibit behavior significantly different from that of consumers who accidentally encounter a brand or product line in the course of broader shopping (search) activity."

24. Amstutz does not specify the functional form he arrived at, or the process of reaching that form. However it appears to be a second degree polynomial rising from 0.05 at the neutral point, to 1.0 at the extreme favorable end.

Summary

A rapid tour through one projection of the largely hidden iceberg of contemporary marketing research is not encouraging—at least, not in the light of some reasonable standards for a sufficient level of knowledge of the predictive value of brand attitudes. These standards were framed as questions to be raised about specific studies, and concerned (1) the desirability of over-time measures at the individual level, (2) some means of representing the brand attitude–brand choice behavior relationship by a functional form, (3) an estimate of the strength of the relationship, and, (4) the identification of the influences on the relationship.

These requirements were satisfied very infrequently in the studies that were reviewed. The principal shortcomings appeared to be (a) the universal use of gross measures of behavior and attitudes, (b) premature and generally excessive aggregation of the data, (c) the dubious but convenient belief that future brand choice behavior is adequately represented by recall of the immediate past, (d) little consideration of the influence of the buying environment on the behavioral manifestation of brand attitudes, and (e) virtually no attempt to explore the deviant cases, that is, to find out why some people buy a brand although they said they were neutral or didn't like it before they bought it.

Other criticisms might be made, but the exercise tends to be self-defeating, because so many of the available studies were designed to solve some other problem. Thus available insights into the brand attitude–subsequent behavior relationship are often gratuitous research fall-out. Also, the empirical performance on this score is not significantly worse than in the other disciplines explored at the beginning of this chapter. But, with this identification of the deficiencies of our present knowledge and some insight into the kinds of relationships and influences to be considered, we have a strong base on which to build this study.

36

Chapter 2

The Relationship of Attitude and Brand Choice Behavior

In this chapter we will explore some of the theoretical considerations in the use of attitudes as predictors of *subsequent* purchase behavior at the *individual level*. To orient the discussion we will first review some conflicting views about the relevance of attitudes as behavioral predispositions. The position will be taken that, in a marketing context, the affective component of brand attitudes has relevance as a predictor if the effects of certain environmental and moderating effects are considered. It is then suggested that the influence of these two factors can be described appropriately within an interpretive framework suggested by a learning process model. In order to link this chapter to the remainder of the study the hypotheses inherent in the model will be summarized along with comments on how they are to be tested. Finally, some implications of the model for marketing strategy will be discussed.

Views of the Relevance of Attitudes as Predictors

In the introductory chapter we saw much evidence that respondents do not always behave consistently in their verbal and action behavior. This evidence has been accumulating (albeit

37

slowly) for some time, and the implications certainly have not been lost to attitude theoreticians. Various theoretical strategies have been suggested to explain this situation—including the argument that the concept of attitude itself is at fault and should be abandoned. An attempt will be made below to evaluate some of the more constructive theoretical strategies in terms of their relevance to buying behavior. The order in which they are discussed is not arbitrary, rather it follows a continuum of increasing relevance.

The Response Consistency Approach

This view is espoused by Green (1954, pages 335–340) in a very influential position paper. Although he claims that his view is consistent with Doob[1] (1947) and Krech and Crutchfield (1948) among others, he seems to have perceived these definitions from a limited, measurement-oriented perspective. Thus he focuses on consistency of response, to a sample of items (stimuli) within a general class, as the basic characteristic of attitudes, de-emphasizing the anticipatory and mediating aspects. Predictive weakness, in Green's view, is unavoidable in the process of sampling from the universe of behaviors in the general class. Because only a sample is used, and we have no way of knowing how representative it is, generalizations are therefore dangerous. Consequently, "one should not make inferences about behavior *other* than verbal responses to similar verbal questions." Bauer's reaction to this seems appropriate, "unquestionably prediction to the same universe as that from which the original construct was inferred is the safest type of activity in which to engage . . . [however] there is little utility to doing this in the case of attitudes" (1966, page 11).

Probability Conceptions

This approach confers predictive power on attitudes by separating the operational from the explanatory problem. This approach has

---

1. Doob's definition is, "an implicit response that is both anticipatory and mediating in reference to patterns of overt responses, that is evoked by a variety of stimulus patterns and that is considered socially insignificant in the individual's society."

been developed the furthest by Campbell (1963), who holds that, "a social attitude is (or is evidenced by) *consistency* in response to social objects." This operational definition makes measurement fairly straightforward, because it only necessitates the recurrence of a certain kind of response to a defined set of attitude questions or attitude objects. Very briefly, the attitude is the manifest responses themselves, not some hypothetical construct or intervening variable.

This hardly seems much of an advance until Campbell establishes that attitudes (along with expectancy, habit, and so forth) are one of a number of acquired—that is, learned—behavioral dispositions. As a matter of fact, attitudes are the most general of the acquired behavioral dispositions as they include both a means or goal construct (in the acquired predisposition to respond) and an ends construct (from the motivational or goal directed quality). Campbell further establishes that, "there is an empirically verifiable relationship between verbal reports in conscious contexts and overt action." The problem of the obvious inconsistency between verbal attitudes and behavior is explained by the presence of "situational threshold differences." That is, people are always consistent with their attitudes within situations having the same threshold value. But new situations will merit response only when the response strength exceeds the situational threshold value. In an economics context aggregate demand would be a function of response strength, and price changes would correspond to shifting the purchase threshold value in the same direction.

This approach provides a robust and useful theoretical basis, but only if one accepts the explanatory definition. The more usual approach argues that attitude measurement directly identifies some latent structure or hidden mechanism. The related overt behavior is also a "manifestation" of this inner and latent structure. This approach is as tentative as Campbell's conception, and it is highly probable that the two are talking about the same thing from different perspectives. However, the latent structure view has developed more strategies for coping with the lack of relationship of attitudes and behavior, and is thus of greater interest.

39

The Latent Structure Conception of Attitude

In the majority of contemporary social psychology textbooks attitude is defined as a concept containing an *affective* or liking component, a *cognitive* or belief component, and a *conative* or action tendency component. The broad acceptance of the multiple component view is due to the theoretical fertility (indeed much of the work on attitude change rests on this definition; see Katz and Stotland, 1959), as well as to the seemingly plausible explanation it provides of the lack of consistency between attitudes and behavior. Fishbein's explanation of the enduring plausibility is useful:

> . . . two people might feel the same amount of affect toward an object but might behave differently with respect to that object, and/or might hold different beliefs about what should be done with respect to that object. Clearly then, since the "action" component is different, these people must have different attitudes. Similarly, two people might be equally favorable toward the object, but they might also have different cognitions about the object; . . . here again they must have different attitudes.[2]

The notion that the intervening state between stimulus and behavior is richer than the affective component has been supported by the work of Osgood *et al.* (1957) on the dimensions of meaning. However, they view attitude as limited to the *evaluative* dimension, or to the summated "affect" toward the various cognitive components. The additional dimensions, which are empirically derived from the factor analysis of semantic differential scales, are called *potency* (or strength) and *activity* (versus passivity). There is no conative dimension or component in this scheme—at least, not as such. The difference between the two concepts of attitude is not great when it is realized that Osgood is more concerned with the characteristics of concepts than with the respondent's predisposition to respond to the concept.

Despite the theoretician's espousal of the multi-component view, most research involving the construction of attitude scales seems to deal only with the affective component or the evaluational dimen-

---

2. Fishbein (1965, page 4).

sion. The reasons are largely practical. A single score makes it much easier to attain the overriding measurement objective of "interindividual comparison with respect to common defined properties" (Scott, 1965). The alternative, multidimensional view, implies that the attitude of any one individual toward an object may fall at any position on three different dimensions.

The Environmental Factors Approach

Characteristically, this approach is less concerned with the content of the latent structure, on the grounds that the inconsistencies between attitudes and behavior are better understood by looking at differences in the circumstances surrounding the observed behavior (DeFleur and Westie 1963). Usually the respondent's verbal behavior in the typical interview situation is free of the coercive forces of everyday life (Hyman 1959). But contrast this relatively standardized interview environment with the range of circumstances that might surround the actual behavior of interest. Not only are there social, legal, and economic constraints to consider, but group and social norms will also be operating to define roles which are very situation-oriented.

Attempts to cope with environmental factors have usually assumed that the underlying latent structure remains constant throughout the encounter with the environment. For example, Rokeach distinguishes between an "attitude-toward-situation" and an "attitude-toward-object," which interact together to determine the observed behavior. Specifically:

. . . a given "attitude-toward-object," whenever activated, need not always be behaviorally manifested or expressed in the same way or to the same degree. Its expression will vary adaptively as the attitude activated by the situation varies, with the attitude-toward-situation *facilitating* or *inhibiting* the expression of attitude-toward-object, and vice versa.[3]

This proposition has many explanatory benefits, but raises some awkward measurement problems within a marketing context; for

---

3. Rokeach (1967, page 532).

example, there are many relevant situational attitudes—some very hard to define, much less measure. Their influence on behavior depends on their relative importance vis-à-vis the attitude-toward-object (or brand in this case). Rokeach suggests that with two attitudes we can use paired comparisons, or educated intuition, to determine the orderings of importance. But by this time we have lost all the general utility of the attitude-toward-object variable.

The Nature of Brand Attitudes: A Synthesis of Viewpoints

We will consider a brand attitude to be a verbal manifestation of a latent structure. This same latent structure is capable of being manifested in different kinds of behavior, depending on the environmental constraints and opportunities, without undergoing any change or rearrangement of content.

Because attitude change theorists (for instance, Rosenberg, 1960) have so persuasively demonstrated the strain for congruency among the attitude components that represent this latent structure, we will also assume that brand attitudes can be (almost) entirely described by a unidimensional measure of the amount of affect toward the brand. In particular we follow the work of Fishbein (1965) in treating cognitions (beliefs about product attributes) and conations (purchase intentions) as indicants of attitudes. Fishbein has demonstrated a high degree of congruence among these components, even in regard to emotion-laden racial attitudes.

Before extending the above conception of brand attitudes, three points must be clarified. First, the latent structure is not entirely "hidden", although it is convenient to treat it this way, given our primary interest in the verbal and behavioral manifestations. To the extent that this latent structure is similar to the hypothetical constructs described by Howard and Sheth (1966), it may include various motives being satisfied by the purchase, the nature of the brands that are considered as worthwhile alternatives, and the

42

decision rules that structure the motives and alternatives. The emphasis on decision rules parallels the social judgment view of attitudes (Sherif, Sherif, and Nebergall, 1965), in which a reaction to a brand requires a judgment which includes an *evaluation* (amount of affect) as well as a *comparison* with other brands. However Sherif *et al.* do not leave the comparison buried in the latent structure, but construct their scales in such a way that it is explicit and contributes to the final evaluation.

Second, we are explicitly distinguishing between a latent structure and a latent process, although the two concepts are often combined. A brand attitude is a description of the affective content of a latent structure. A latent process is a dynamic change in a latent structure, such as a rearrangement of the components or an addition to or a subtraction from the total content (see Miller, 1965).

Third, by viewing intentions as congruent with the measures of affect, because they are both representations of the same latent structure, we are assuming that there are no barriers to the achievement of this congruency that are influencing the *buyers* of the product. This would seem to be particularly true of the kind of uninvolving attitudes formed by the process of incidental learning, as suggested by Krugman (1965).

The limitation of the congruency condition to buyers of the product class is very important. The classic example of incongruency can be found between the attitudes and the intentions to buy of an average person toward Rolls-Royce cars. However, this is a very misleading example, as the average person is not in the market for luxury cars; this is all his intentions tell us.

However, there is a widespread feeling within marketing that intentions do differ from attitudes (measures of affect) by "combining a consumer's regard for the item with an assessment of its purchase probability" (Wells, 1961, page 82). To this writer's knowledge no one has tested this notion using brand attitudes and intentions. Somewhat related work, dealing with the forecasting of durables expenditures, has found on several occasions that intentions do not improve the forecasts once attitudinal variables have

43

been incorporated. The answer to these differing points of view possibly lies in the generality of the assumption concerning the lack of barriers.[4] For example, if a respondent has a high regard for a number of brands she may use a decision rule to select one of them that is too subtle to be distinguished on the attitude scale. In this case the intentions measure might be a useful supplementary predictor of brand choice behavior. Intentions will probably provide a better prediction in situations where the buyer whose attitude is elicited is merely carrying out the request of someone else who is the actual user. The extent to which intentions are better than measures of affect when there are multiple users will depend on the ability of the family decision process to achieve a consensus of all members of the family. Given the uncertainty surrounding this issue there is a clear need for empirical verification of the assumption whenever it is used.

So far we have established one general property of an attitude toward a brand: namely, that it is a measure of affect and thus has either a favorable or unfavorable direction. The second most important property is the degree of favorableness or unfavorableness. This is generally regarded to be continuously varying along a scale, although usually measured by discrete categories. Together these properties define the *polarity* of the attitude.

Variability In Strength of Motives

Knowledge of the polarity of an attitude toward an object provides only partial information about the strength of motives relevant to behavior toward that object. According to Peak (1955), "only the evaluative reaction portion of the total motive strength varies directly with the polarity of the attitude." Beyond this, there are two, more general motive properties which are also a part of the latent structure. The first is "arousal value," or strength of

---

4. It is difficult to say whether intentions or affect will be better predictors of new product or new brand purchase. The former has the advantage of isolating cases of pure curiosity leading to trial. However, both measures are likely to be based on very little information.

feeling or *involvement* with the attitude object. Involvement may be thought of in terms of the general level of interest in the object, or the centrality of the object to the person's ego-structure. Current evidence indicates that this property may often be only weakly related to the polarity of the attitude (Weksel and Hennes, 1965). A second and somewhat related motive property is described by the person's *confidence* in his attitude judgments. Depending on the circumstances, the degree of confidence could reflect either uncertainty as to which judgment is correct, or ambiguity as to the meaning of the attitude object (Zajonc and Morrisett, 1960).

The key feature of the motive properties of involvement and confidence is that, together, they determine the stability of the observed attitude. And, as the Sherifs (1965) have found in their studies of attitude change and ego-involvement, it is this quality that largely determines the ease with which the attitude can be changed.[5]

Scott also discusses some other properties which are primarily relevant to discussions of the multiple-component view, such as ambivalence (the presence of favorable and unfavorable components), affective salience (degree of contribution of each of the three components), overtness (prominence of the conative component), and consciousness of the attitude.

The Complexity of Purchase Behavior

The specification of the behavioral manifestation of the latent structure would seem to be a straightforward problem. Yet it can be argued (Beldo, 1961) that because overt behavior is attitude turned inside out, it should be scaled and analyzed as precisely as attitudes. The familiar measurement criteria of reliability, sensitivity, and validity can be applied to brand choice decisions (primarily where repeat purchasing is involved) to suggest an appropriate measure of behavior.

---

5. Stability is closely related to cognitive complexity, "The richness of the ideational content or the number of ideas the person has about the object" (Scott, 1965).

A *reliable* measure of purchase behavior implies cumulative, over-time measures where possible. Single purchases, particularly of frequently used food products, are too susceptible to random influences to be useful as predictive criteria at the individual level. It should be noted that this might not hold true at the aggregate level because of off-setting effects. The solution followed here will be to consider brand choice behavior as a latent probabilistic process, subject to the condition that some purchase of the product class[6] be made. The higher the probability, the more intense the behavior, and the less the response to competing brands. A simple and practical estimator of this probability is the cumulative proportion of the total product purchases, devoted to the brand being analyzed, during a significant time period. The estimate will be unbiased on the average if there are no strong brand share trends or significant innovative changes in the market (Ehrenberg, 1966). However, there is no guarantee that the probability will be constant throughout the time period as the buyer's experience accumulates (Carman and Stromberg, 1967). In general, as *sensitivity* is improved by considering more purchases the reliability will also improve, because the measure will include more experience.

A *valid* measure of purchase behavior is also difficult to obtain, for validating here is not the usual process of confirming existence (as by this definition behavior must be valid), but of making sure that something else is not being measured. There are many possible behaviors associated with acquiring a brand, that might be predicted from brand attitudes. Himmelstrand (1960) has proposed several categories of behavior that precede the commonly used *congruent* (that is, actual purchase) act: (1) "*Symbol* acts, which have symbols as their exclusive objects." This includes the communicative acts predicted by personal influence theories, including talking about, criticizing, and praising the brand; and (2) "*Referent* acts (other than actual behavior), which are preoccupied with the referents of

---

6. A possible source of error can arise in the way individuals classify the product class. To cite a well-known difficulty in the coffee market, the purchase of Sanka might be a *complement* to the purchase of Yuban to one buyer, while another may treat them as direct substitutes.

that verbal attitude by way of learning to know it, manipulating it and/or consuming it." A whole series of acts are suggested here, including searching out information from friends and advertisements, consuming or trying the brand outside the home, going to the showroom (see Smith, 1965), looking for the brand on the shelf in order to price it and compare it with other brands, and so forth. It seems that none of these is likely to be consistently more valid than purchasing, because few can be consistently applied to all product categories, the measures are necessarily gross, and there is the constant danger that when social interaction is involved the measures will include more general social processes. Finally, even if purchasing behavior were not the most valid, it is by all odds the most immediately useful to study.

A Model of the Relationship of Brand Attitudes and Brand Choice Behavior

The nature of the attitudes and behavior we are studying suggests that an appropriate model of their relationship must satisfy four conditions: It must (a) incorporate a unidimensional measure of overall affect toward a specific brand, (b) relate this attitude to a reliable and valid over-time measure of subsequent purchase behavior, (c) consider the influence of the environment on the behavioral manifestation of the latent structure, and (d) take into account individual differences in the stability of attitudes, and hence in the ease with which they may be changed.

The key to the model is the treatment of environmental influences. We have already identified one role of the environment in the form of an attitude-toward-situation which either facilitates or inhibits the specific attitude toward the brand. Essentially the attitude-toward-situation is a device to summarize the many forms of coercive forces that the buyer may encounter. For the kind of behavior that marketers want to predict the most obvious forces

47

are the relative attraction of competing brands, the brand preferences of family and friends, and the buyer's appraisal of the kind of social behavior that is appropriate to the purchasing or using situation.

There is a second possibility that the *actual* environment may be different from the *expected* environment (at the time the attitude was elicited). This problem is at the heart of the marketing research function, for it deals with the response of the buyer to something new in the environment: a deal, a new brand, a short-term out-of-stock of a familiar brand, conversations with salesmen, a new advertising campaign (including point-of-purchase displays), and so forth. These encounters can lead either to attitude change, or to mere acceptance as temporary disruptions that do not justify a change in attitude. Regardless of whether the change in environment is internalized as an attitude change, the effect, once again, will be to inhibit or facilitate the expression of the original "attitude-toward-object," as well as the behavior toward the object.

In a more general sense the encounter with the environment will lead to either momentary or possibly long-term learning—defined here as a systematic strengthening, weakening, or eliminating, of the latent structure directing overt behavior. The direction of effect of this learning will depend on the initial attitude. Thus, when the initial attitude is extremely favorable, the learning cannot increase the likelihood that the buyer will choose the brand (because it was previously at a maximum), and may well reduce it. Conversely, an extremely unfavorable attitude toward a brand might still lead to some subsequent choices under certain conditions, for instance, if the brand started heavy dealing or couponing to reduce the restraining effect of price or the favored brand was out-of-stock. The first effect of the environment that is described above is an *inhibiting* one, while the second is *facilitating*.

The Nature of the Model

The basic *inputs* to the model are assumed to be an interval scale measure of a brand attitude at one point in time, and an estimate of the probability of purchasing the brand during a subsequent period of time (this probability is conditional on purchase of the product class). The damping effects of the environment that are described above can be most efficiently portrayed by specifying the relationship in a functional form. For convenience we will assume the relationship is linear, although any monotonic function would serve just as well.

(1) $P\{K|P\}_i = \alpha - \beta A_i + u_i$ $\qquad\qquad i = 1, \ldots N$

where: $P\{K|P\}_i =$ The estimated probability of person i buying brand K, given the purchase of product P, in the fixed time period considered.

$A_i =$ The *initial* attitude of person i toward brand A. This measure is scaled so that a very favorable attitude has a low score.

(2) $\beta = f$ (inhibiting and facilitating effects of the environment, when estimated over all N buyers of the product).

(3) $u_i = f$ (stability of attitude, buying style, extraneous determinants of response, nature of the environment encountered, and random error).[7]

Equation (3) provides a specific recognition that buyers with the same initial evaluation may respond differently to similar environmental influences (deals, price changes, promotions, displays, out-of-stocks, and so forth) encountered during the time

---

7. Equation (3) could have been added to equation (1) as direct interaction terms, and the interpretation would have been the same. Thus, if we were interested in a single effect, such as stability (measured by a variable X_1), the equation could be written:

$$P\{K|P\}_i = a + b_1 A_2 + b_2 X_1 + c I_{AX_1} + e$$

where I_{AX_1} is a first-order interaction term and e is the random error. This approach was not used because the large number of possible interaction terms would make the equation very unmanageable. Also the β, parameter could not have been interpreted as suggested by the model if the additional terms were included (Blalock and Blalock, 1968).

49

period being studied. In part, the differences in response will depend on the stability of the initial attitude. As discussed above, buyers with very stable attitudes will be less influenced by the environment they encounter. There is the further possibility that the person's "buying style" will have much the same effect. Here we are thinking of the variety of trait-like characteristics of buyers, such as perceived impulsiveness, innovativeness, and economy consciousness, that have been recently developed to explain various facets of buying behavior (Pessemier, Burger, and Tigert, 1967). Such measures fit logically into this model, because they also provide information about differences in responses to similar environmental influences. Equation (3) also accounts for differences in the environmental influences encountered. For example, not all buyers will encounter the same proportion of out-of-stocks. Finally, some consideration must be given to consistent biases in response, due to yea-saying and so forth.

AN INTERPRETIVE FRAMEWORK

To make it clear how the environmental influences are incorporated into the model it is useful to look at a conceptual framework adapted from stochastic learning theory (see Bush and Mosteller, 1955, for example).[8] The starting point is the hypothetical situation of isomorphism between attitudes and subsequent choice behavior portrayed in Figure 2–1. The hypothetical situation represents either no environmental influences, *or* a group of buyers who are completely impervious to environmental influences in the time interval studied. As soon as these hypothetical conditions are removed, the damping influence of the environment is felt. The extent of this influence is represented by

8. This class of models is usually employed to study a single stochastic measure of behavior that is mediated by some environmental condition (which may be inhibiting or facilitating or both) and can be generalized to n time periods. When only one time period is considered this model is also appropriate to describe the transformation of a deterministic variable (attitude) into a stochastic variable (behavior) in the presence of various environmental influences. For other marketing applications of this model see Kuehn (1962), Farley and Kuehn (1965), Carmen (1965), Massy (1965), and Haines (1964).

the size of the slope parameter, β. When β is small, prior knowledge of a buyer's brand attitude contributes very little information about subsequent behavior. Or, to put it another way, behavior is largely determined by conditions at the time of purchase. This is likely to be the situation when the repurchase cycle is long, in which case the initial attitude may not be relevant to the new purchasing environment, or when the product is close to becoming a commodity and brand judgments are difficult to make because of the lack of meaningful brand differentiation. To complete the picture, it should be noted that the stability of the attitude (represented by the degree of confidence and interest) ultimately influences both the *dispersion* (u_i) and the *slope* (β) of the relationship, because it determines the extent of the response to environmental influences.

The actual relationship shown in Figure 2–1 is not intended to portray any particular brand or product class. It does suggest a situation in which the facilitating effects of the environment (*a* parameter) are relatively more influential than the inhibiting

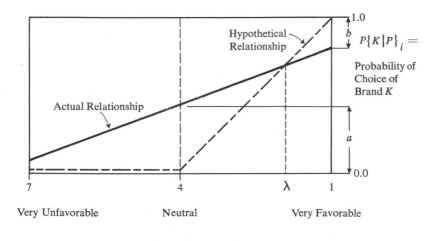

Figure 2–1. Basic attitude-behavior model.

effects (b parameter). There are several practical constraints to the values that the a and b parameters can take. The actual sizes of the two parameters are most influenced by the *elevation* of the relationship, which in turn is a function of the number of brands in the market. In general, the fewer important brands there are in a product market, the higher the probable elevation. The relative sizes of the two parameters are constrained in one direction by the assumption that the worst predictive situation is represented by a horizontal relationship. This is the case where brand choice is entirely determined by the environment at the time of purchase, and attitudes contribute no useful information. Finally, it is very unlikely that the a parameter would be very large relative to the b parameter. In markets with two or three other large brands, such a situation would imply that the brand being studied had taken over the market.

INSIGHTS INTO ATTITUDE CHANGE

The model does not explicitly distinguish between the damping effects of the environment which lead to attitude change versus those that are merely momentary disruptions. However, to the extent that there is true attitude change the direction can be inferred from the model as a shift away from extreme attitude positions. This inference could be checked after one or more purchase decisions by a follow-up interview. The initial (I_a) and follow-up (F_a) attitudes would tend to shift as follows:

$I_a \longrightarrow F_a$	Mean Attitude	$F_a \longleftarrow I_a$
Extremely Unfavorable	Neutral	Extremely Favorable

This regression toward the mean has often been observed in panel designs (Campbell and Clayton, 1961). Usually regression is attributed to errors of measurement or response unreliability, but in this situation there are specific environmental pressures that favor this tendency. Such regression effects should be interpreted with discretion, because they only represent average tendencies. There are many buyers, particularly those whose attitudes are very stable, who are not likely to shift at all. A further complicating feature is the fact that the pool of buyers is constantly being depleted and replenished. Ruch (1966) has shown that for some product classes this buyer flow—rather than brand switching—is the major source of change in volume. Under these conditions considerable care must be taken in the definition of a buyer for this analysis of attitude change.

When the model is applied to a series of brand choices in a product class with a short repurchase cycle, during a period of several months, it becomes apparent that there will be no change in the latent structure between most pairs of choices, although one or more permanent changes may take place at some point in a long sequence of choices. For one reason, new promotional activity is scheduled on a monthly or quarterly basis in many product categories, so there is a high degree of week-to-week similarity in the purchasing environment. More important, most buyers make so many brand choice decisions during a month that it would be highly uncomfortable to have to adjust each latent structure on a frequent basis. In the interests of comfort and consistency buyers have developed a number of stratagems to shut out disruptive information. It is this consistency that we rely upon when making predictions about choice behavior from brand attitudes. However, when the repurchase cycle is very long there is no need for such consistency between purchases, with the result that brand attitudes are not likely to be good predictors of behavior.

Limitations of the Model

(a) *The availability of suitable measures of attitude and behavior.* First, there is the question of the interval nature of the *attitude scale*. Although this problem has received the intermittent attention of attitude researchers for at least thirty years it is far from being resolved (for the basic measurement issues, see Coleman, 1964: Chapter 2). Since the answer to the question depends somewhat on the type of scale used, we will defer a review of the evidence until the scales are developed in the specific testing situations. We basically take the position that objective means of distributing respondents along an equal-interval scale of affect are available, and have sufficient validity and reliability. A more troublesome issue is the increasing inadequacy of the probability measure of *behavior* as the purchase cycle lengthens. Reference to a chart of confidence limits for proportions (Richmond, 1964, page 585), shows that the proportion of purchases devoted to a brand is a poor estimator of the true probability when the average number of brand choices is less than ten or fifteen (during the finite period being studied). When a good estimate is available the appropriate procedure is to fit a series of polynomials to the individual attitude and probability scores. However, when the average number of purchases may be only one or two, as with durable goods, some degree of aggregation is necessary. Because attitude is the predictor variable, any aggregation should be confined to groups that are homogeneous as far as initial attitude is concerned. This aggregation might be limited to cells of five or ten persons holding the same attitude, or might extend to every respondent with the same attitude. With semi-aggregation it is still possible to fit polynomials to each "within-cell" attitude and behavior measure. The major drawback is the possibility that basically unlike people may be classified together in a single cell, in which case the results would be very sensitive to manipulations of cell sizes and composition. A safer approach is to aggregate across all respondents having the same initial attitude. While a great deal of information on the form of the attitude–behavior relationship is lost by this approach, it is still possible to test for the presence of a monotonically increasing relationship. Instead of requiring the purchase probability to increase monotonically as attitude improves, the test would be confined to relating more favorable attitudes to increasing proportions of buyers of the brand among all buyers. The presence of monotonicity could be demonstrated by a chi-square test.

(*b*) *General shortcomings of the panel design.* The reliability and validity of the results may be affected by problems of sample composition and mortality, respondent sensitization to the brands or products being studied, recording accuracy, and so forth. The

54

available evidence, which shows that these problems do not seem to influence basic relationships, is reviewed in Appendix A.

(*c*) *The assumption of linearity of isomorphism in the absence of environmental factors.* The problem centers on the motivating quality of a change in affect. A generalization of Weber's law (see Berelson and Steinger, page 97) would suggest that the stimulus of increasing affect is likely to be manifested in a proportionately larger behavior response, according to some kind of exponential weighting.

(*d*) *The nature of the market.* Because of the nature of the data required, the model may only be applied to relatively stable markets with at least two or three major brands. When there is only one brand of any note, that is, with more than 70 per cent of the market, or a new brand had been introduced that ultimately accounted for a significant part of the total sales during the period under study, it is not possible to estimate purchase probabilities. These conditions are not too restrictive, as they apply to relatively few markets at any one point in time.

Testing the Model

Although this model represents the resultant effect of many environmental influences, it only requires knowledge of two unidimensional variables. However, satisfying this minimum condition is not a sufficient condition for a test of the model, because it only permits a description of the relationship. A crude test is possible if data on attitudes and subsequent behavior is available for two product classes with very different repurchase cycles. In this testing situation the focus would be on the slope (β) of the relationship. The rationale for this kind of a test will be discussed in the next section, dealing with ways to account for differences in the repurchase cycle.

A more sensitive test involves the segmentation of the buyers into groups, such that there is maximum between-group variation in the extent of reaction to environmental influences. The appropriate segmentation dimensions are the two most significant variables in the equation estimating u_i, the residual of the attitude–behavior relationship. The goal of this method is to obtain maximum variability in the slope and dispersion of the predictive relationship. In particular the relationship for the segment that demonstrated the least reaction to the environment should have the steepest slope and the least dispersion.

A third possibility for a test hinges on the ability of the model to predict the type of reaction to the environment. Specifically, buyers with initial attitudes more favorable than λ constitute a group who were either inhibited or not affected by environment factors. By contrast those buyers of the brand whose initial attitude was less favorable than λ responded to the facilitating aspects of the environment. Had this latter group been inhibited by the environment there would be no reason for them to buy the brand —even though they bought other brands in the product class. We already know a great deal about such factors as exposure to new information, opportunity to make a brand choice, price, and financial constraints and family decisions processes, for they have been studied in many contexts. A part of Chapter 3 will be devoted to reviewing relevant evidence about these environmental factors.

Illustrative Applications of the Model

ACCOUNTING FOR THE EFFECT OF THE LENGTH OF REPURCHASE CYCLE

Many conceptual approaches have been used to compare the purchase decision for products with long repurchase cycles (in particular, appliances) with those having short repurchase cycles (the majority of non-durables). Differences in decision processes have been attributed to characteristics of the stage of learning (Howard, 1963), the perceived risk of the purchase (Bauer, 1960), the need for pre-purchase deliberation (Katona and Mueller,

1955), or the influence of habit (Pratt, 1965, page 121). These approaches agree that the important dimensions on which to look for differences are the amount of thinking involved, the actual time consumed in the decision, the extent of circumspectness, the number of alternatives considered, and the extent of information seeking from personal and impersonal sources.

For our purposes the most insightful explanation is that, as the purchase cycle *shortens*, the knowledge and attitudes gained from previous experience (both shopping and usage) become increasingly relevant to subsequent brand choice decisions. There are three sources of prior knowledge and attitudes:

(*a*) *From satisfaction or dissatisfaction with past usage.* In the event the purchase was satisfying, the initial brand attitude will certainly be reinforced. If the experience was not entirely satisfactory, or satisfaction is hard to evaluate, cognitive dissonance theory suggests a number of possible outcomes, including attitude change and/or search for information or rationalizations to support the initial decision (Festinger, 1957). But regardless of what took place after the purchase, the outcome is more likely to be remembered if it took place recently (the specification of how "recently" will vary considerably by product class).

(*b*) *From updating the knowledge of the state of the environment.* Generally speaking,[9] the more often a buyer shops for a product the more likely she is to be well versed in the brands and product features currently available, the range of prices to be expected, the stores where the best value can be found and so forth. If she has never shopped for the product before, her knowledge and opinions may be based on little more than unrelated messages from mass media and some feeling for the experience of friends or family.

(*c*) *From opportunities for "behavioral completion".* Krugman has recently shown that when involvement in brand advertising is low, the effect of the message may be long delayed or lost

---

9. This deserves qualification in very short purchase cycle situations where each decision is often entirely habitual and considers little new information.

depending on the probability that the following sequence takes place,[10]

(a) . . . there ensues an unstable condition characterized by a shift in perceptual structure without a corresponding shift in attitudinal structure. (b) A behavioral opportunity, such as in-store shopping, triggers the potential for shift in perceptual structure. (c) Behavioral completion releases appropriate attitudes supportive and consistent with the shift in perceptual structure, i.e. if the brand is then purchased the new way of seeing it may then for the first time be expressed in words, for example, to "explain" why it was selected.[11]

The new effect of behavioral completion, in conjunction with usage experience is to establish more stable, firmer attitudes.

In the context of the model, we can reinterpret the above to say that as the repurchase cycle shortens, the influence of the environmental factors on the attitude–behavior relationship is steadily lessened, because (1) there is a greater backlog of remembered experience with the brand and the product; (2) there is better prior knowledge of the environmental factors that will be encountered during the shopping process; and (3) the attitudes themselves are more stable and less likely to change under normal circumstances. It follows, that when the influence of the environmental factors has been reduced to a minimum, that purchase behavior will achieve maximum isomorphism with initial attitudes and the slope will be the steepest. Or to put it another way, initial attitudes will then provide maximum information about subsequent behavior. On the other hand, as the purchase cycle *lengthens* to the point where the purchase is a one-time event, there is considerable deliberation and information seeking, little prior knowledge of the nature of the environment, no feedback from previous experience and, generally, a paucity of knowledge on which to base an attitude. We would expect, in this extreme case, that initial attitudes would be poor predictors of subsequent brand choices.

---

10. According to Krugman, if advertising involvement is high, the effect on attitude will be the same as suggested by the operation of the environmental factors.

11. Krugman (1967, page 585).

INSIGHTS INTO BRAND LOYALTY

Newman (1966, page 16) has noted that our understanding of brand loyalty does not extend much beyond an awareness that buying is not a random process, ". . . the definition of loyalty, which typically has been used, specifies only that a certain percentage of a household's purchases go to one brand within a given time period. It says nothing about whether the purchaser feels an attachment to the brand, and, if so, how strong the feeling is." Apropos of this criticism the model provides a more realistic measure of loyalty, since it concentrates on proportion of brand purchase decisions, and relates this measure to the prior degree of "attachment."

This two dimensional view of loyalty, which requires an understanding of the interplay of attitude and behavior, appears more insightful than the usual behavioristic view based entirely on the proportion of total purchases. This approach will be more fully developed in Chapter 6.

COMPARISON OF THE SLOPE OF THE RELATIONSHIP BETWEEN BRANDS AND BETWEEN TIME PERIODS

Because the model is not influenced by the numbers of people within an attitude or purchase category, we can say, as a first approximation, that the slope and shape of the predictive relationship does not depend on the share of the market.[12] That being the case, we can compare the curves for each of the major brands in the market, to determine which brand is most successful in exploiting a favorable predisposition or overcoming neutral or unfavorable attitudes.[13] Also, of course, we can estimate improvement or decline over long periods of time. Both of these possible applications are useful as management controls, in that they pinpoint weakness in each brand's position.

---

12. The anomaly of popularity and liking (see McPhee, 1963) might cause problems in this respect. Also recall that elevation is a function of the number of brands in the market.

13. For an example of this general approach, see Pratt (1965).

SOURCE OF SALES

By plotting the proportion of the total buyers of the product, in each category of attitude and probability of purchase of the brand, along the two axes of the model, we can see at a glance where most of each brand's buyers are coming from. Clearly the higher the *average* probability of purchases and the *average* initial attitude the stronger the position of the brand. As these average values decline the position of the brand becomes increasingly vulnerable because sales are more dependent on the buyer's response to such environmental factors as price level or deal frequency. Before we can determine which of these factors are liable to be most influential, we must learn more about them. This is the task of the next chapter.

Chapter 3

Influences on the Attitude— Behavior Relationship

The mainspring of the model of buyer attitudes and brand choice behavior presented in Chapter 2 is the notion that overt behavior is the consequence of the joint effects of an underlying latent structure (which can be partially elicited by attitude measures), and the state of the environment at the time of the purchase. In particular the model provides for the effects of either a momentary adaptation or a more enduring learning experience from the encounter with the environment. Up to this point, we have only talked about environmental factors in general terms. Yet, for testing the model and determining the relative importance of the factors that the marketer is able to influence, is it essential to be able to describe the environment encountered by each buyer in reasonably specific terms. The question of which descriptors to use is the first issue investigated in this chapter.

As we noted earlier, it would be unwise to expect that a description of the initial attitude and subsequent environmental influences would provide complete information about subsequent behavior. A further purpose of this chapter is to identify possible "moderating effects" that reduce the predictive strength of the

---

1. Hereafter we will use the term "attitude–behavior relationship" in place of the more accurate, but cumbersome term "prior attitude–subsequent brand choice behavior relationship."

model. Here we will be concerned with individual differences in attitude stability and buying style.

The testing strategy appropriate to understanding the role of the environmental factors is in the tradition of the "known group method" or more generally, "the analytical approach . . . to the empirical analysis of action" (Lazarsfeld, 1959, page 104). The core of the analysis is the comparison of *buyers of a brand* who were (probably) inhibited with those who were (probably) facilitated by the environmental factors. To the extent that these two groups differ in the presence or absence of explanatory variables that describe the environment that the buyers most likely encountered in the buying process we can infer the influence of environmental factors on the relationship. If a simultaneous multivariate comparison procedure is used we may further infer the relative influence of each environmental factor compared to all the others.

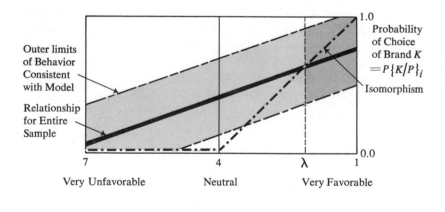

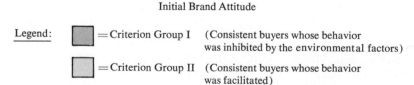

Initial Brand Attitude

Figure 3–1. Influence of moderating effects and environmental factors.

62

The moderating or error producing effects do create some problems in the interpretation of this analysis. These moderating effects can be separately singled out according to their influence on the size of the residual of the attitude–behavior relationship. However when it comes to looking at environmental factors the only way to neutralize the influence of the moderating effects, on the difference between criterion groups that were facilitated or inhibited, is to limit the analysis to those buyers who are consistent with the model. Empirically this means setting limits on the extent of deviation from the estimated attitude–behavior relationship, as shown in Figure 3–1. Within the limits shown, the response pattern is assumed to be determined primarily by the reaction to the environment.

In summary then, it is the purpose of this chapter to specify variables that may have a significant effect on the attitude–behavior relationship. Their influence will be inferred from their differential presence in several criterion groups. Further insights will be gained by contrasting the role and influence of the variables in two different purchasing contexts: appliances, and regularly purchased food products.

The Role of Environmental Factors

Each of these factors is anchored in some way to the personal or shopping environment encountered during the decision-making process. This includes exposure to new information, the competitive effect of similar brands, interferences from price, lack of availability, time pressure, overall financial constraints, and the influence of family decision processes. Each of these environmental factors will be described in enough detail that an appraisal of the nature and direction of effect can be made. The coverage certainly will not be exhaustive, as each separate factor has spawned a large and usually controversial literature. Unless otherwise noted, their effect will be to dampen the behavioral manifestation of the latent

63

process. We will focus somewhat more on the features of the environment that facilitate some behavioral manifestation from an initially unfavorable or neutral latent process (as it is represented by the brand attitude). As a consequence, most of the discussion will be in terms of Criterion Group II in Figure 3–1, as this group encompasses those buyers of the brand who were facilitated by the environment.

Exposure to New Information

This exposure could either be *induced,* as when information is actively sought, or passively accepted—assuming it is not ignored. In either case the buyer learns a new perspective or set of cognitions about the product class and the brands available. When the purchase cycle is very long, as in washing machines, the buyer may be completely re-educated by new information about the brands available, new performance features, and relevant criteria for appraisal. In this case previous knowledge is largely obsolete. For food products with short purchase cycles the new information may be limited to up-dating the price and deal structure for the brand, and reacting to the occasional new slogan, flavor, or package.

The new information may be of so little consequence that it is not internalized, despite having a momentary impact on a single purchase decision. Several possibilities were suggested earlier to explain the effect of new information that is internalized. In line with Krugman's work the effect might be limited to restructuring the pattern of attribute saliency. This assumes great importance when there are no obvious physical criteria for judging a product and advertising is a source of information about criteria. As an extreme example, consumers of soft drinks did not become concerned with calory content until this dimension was emphasized through the introduction of new brands and very specific advertising. However, a more probable effect of new information is an actual attitude change in order to maintain congruity between affect and cognition.[2]

---

2. By employing a balance model here we are implicity assuming that brand

This prediction about the effect of new information on the attitude–behavior relationship is similar to a prediction based on the economics of information (Stigler, 1961), when applied to the problem of brand loyalty (Farley, 1964a, page 370), "If, under such a theory brands are generally considered good substitutes for one another, then households which put considerable effort into gathering market information should appear less brand loyal toward all products than those families which search very little." In terms of the model discussed here, Criterion Group II is less brand loyal, and moreover, only purchased because of the extra effort put into gathering information.

This suggests a variety of possible measures on which to contrast the two criterion groups. Ideally we could measure efforts made to obtain information (as represented by number of stores visited, number of product features considered, discussions with friends and salesmen, length of time spent, and so forth) or actual exposure to new information about the brands. Usually, to avoid contaminating the deliberation process, we will have to make indirect inferences. For example we would expect Criterion Group II to be more broadly exposed to media, more interested in shopping activities and shopping oriented information, and less constrained because of the time pressure.[3] From work by Mueller (1954), on the degree of deliberation and information seeking that entered into the purchase of a durable good, we would expect Criterion Group II to be younger and at an earlier stage in the family life cycle. Also Coulson (1966, page 65) suggests, "that there are times in a person's life when he is more apt to change products and brands than at other times." Some of these relate to the family life cycle, such as the addition of children; others, such as moves,

---

attitudes primarily serve a knowledge function, "as a basis for structuring and interpreting events," (Katz 1960) and that the expression of an attitude only represents a respondent's effort to *externalize* what he believes privately (Smith, Bruner, and White, 1956, page 41).

3. According to Caplovitz (1965) poor people are very likely to buy what they know best, or what is readily available, because there is invariably a pressing need for the item.

usually precipitate many purchases in a somewhat changed information environment. All of these variables clearly have more relevance in the case of appliances, where the information needs are greater. This is consistent with the earlier suggestion that the impact of the environmental factors is a function of the product purchase cycle.

Opportunity to Make a Brand Choice

The establishment and maintenance of full distribution is the constant concern of all consumer products manufacturers. In company with retailers, they realize that lack of availability of their brand is the fastest way to lose a sale. As products are designed to satisfy increasingly segmented markets, product availability has had to extend to encompass all kinds of product features, colors, sizes, flavors, and other options. Lack of any of these options may lead the buyer to look at other, previously unconsidered brands.

Within the framework of the model, availability can have a facilitating or an inhibiting effect. The *inhibiting* effect, which results when a person buys another brand because the favored brand is not available, is most familiar. Of course, to the brand purchased this is a *facilitating* effect. As Moulson (1965, page 57) warns us, the act of buying a brand because it is the only one available leads to a spurious conclusion about the extent of brand loyalty. Then we have a situation where, "it is the arithmetic chances of being bought which, in the absence of consumer preference, predetermine the market share and rate of repurchasing a brand will enjoy." This is most likely to occur when the repurchase cycle is short, there are only a few brands in the category, and the purchase is not important enough to justify looking any further.[4] As the repurchase cycle lengthens, the marketer's emphasis shifts to ensuring that the buyer will encounter the brand

---

4. However, buyers do react differently to the unavailability of the brand they want. Peckham (1963) reports that 58 per cent of buyers would accept a substitute brand if the one they wanted was not available. This percentage varied widely for different grocery products, but was never more than 70 per cent.

during the search process that precedes the decision. In this case, as the selection of brands increases, the buyer is more likely to buy a previously unconsidered brand because he has learned that it is best for his needs. Of course, he might also buy this brand because it was the only one available.

The only truly satisfactory way of incorporating the effects of lack of availability into the model is to describe each person according to his actual experience. Then we would expect that Criterion Group II bought an unfavorably rated brand of food product because it was the only one available. This is less likely for appliances. Rather, we would expect that Criterion Group II was exposed to a greater selection of brands, which facilitated the reappraisal of unfavorably rated brands.

We are usually prevented from gaining such detailed and immediate knowledge of each purchase. This unfortunately means that we have to fall back on some weak inferences. For example, in the case of food products we would expect buyers who patronize small stores in rural areas to be strongly influenced by the inhibiting effects of availability. But with appliances these same rural buyers will not likely have a wide selection of brands to consider. Then we would predict that they would be less likely to buy a previously unfavored brand, because they did not have the opportunity to find out whether it really was better for their needs. These inferences are weak, because describing a person as a city or country dweller implies much more than the number of brands available to chose from. Among other things it has a bearing on the effect of price, which is another environmental factor to consider. But first we must consider the related problem of the presence of other equally attractive brands.

The Influence of Competing Brands

A market has been defined as,

. . . the inter-related class of brands or products whose relations of substitution and competition are powerful enough so that the sales of each are strongly influenced by the sales of others. In econometric language a market, for our purposes, would be the set of items whose cross-elasticities of demand exhibited sufficiently powerful substitution effects.[5]

This definition has the virtue of forcing us back to the awkward reality where successful brands (and politicians) are rapidly copied in the expectation that success is transferable. Even if this were not the case, no marketing strategist would long permit his brand to be regarded as consistently inferior to the competition. The net result is that the buyer is often in the position of having to choose one of several equally desirable alternatives.[6] Since we assume that a choice is ultimately made, some kind of a decision rule must be used. Even granting that different people may use different decision rules when faced with the same situation, it is to the discredit of the empirical work on brand loyalty that we still know very little about these decision rules. About all that can be said is that the choice is not entirely random. In the coffee market, where brand differentiation is often slight and diminishing with time, the pattern of purchases is surprisingly close to that predicted by a random Poisson process (Coleman, 1965, page 322). But if the process is not random, and we hold the effect of other environmental factors constant, we are left with the possibility that the choice is governed (1) by habit, periodically interrupted by the desire for change (as suggested by Howard and Sheth, 1966); (2) by what everyone else does, (Miller and Starr, 1960, page 189), or (3) that dissonance over the inability to choose leads to the espousal (or invention) of reasons why one brand is better than another.

In some ways the discussion of choice between equally preferred alternatives is a caricature. In many markets the strategies of product differentiation or segmentation have been successful, the ability to discriminate among brands varies widely among buyers, and the pressure on retail space is such that there is often only room for one of a pair of close substitutes.

So far as the model under discussion is concerned, the effect of

---

5. Stefflre (1965, page 2).

6. This is a logical outcome that is predictable from Thurstone's (1945) early work on choice among competing alternatives. It is contrary to what we would expect from successful product differentiation or market segmentation (Smith 1956, for example).

other brands is entirely *inhibiting*. That is, while this environmental factor inhibits the purchase of highly regarded brands that have close substitutes, it cannot improve the prospects of any brands that were previously unfavored (unless there is an improvement in the attitude toward these latter brands for some other reason). Consequently we can only look to the shape of the curve describing the attitude–behavior relationship to understand the influence. We would expect that as the number of close substitutes in the market increases, the segment of the curve to the right of λ will become flatter. This corresponds to the empirical finding that consumers, ". . . tended to be less loyal toward products with many brands available . . . and where market share is not concentrated heavily in the leading brand" (Farley, 1964b, page 14).

The Effect of the Store Environment

We have seen that buyers tend to shop at several stores to obtain information about products with long repurchase cycles. It has also been found that buyers of grocery and drug products will often routinely shop at several stores, in the course of expanding their selection or looking for special prices. The question here is whether a change in the store environment will lead to a different brand choice decision, even though the underlying latent structure relevant to brand attitudes is unchanged. In extreme cases the answer is obviously yes; as when a person makes one brand choice decision in a self-service store, and the next in an exclusive store with the help of a knowledgeable clerk. The behavior will obviously vary to some extent because different selections of brands will be available. But beyond this there are other environmental influences that will cause brand choice behavior to vary adaptively.

Stores do have different images, and engender different levels of trust,[7] because of their average price level, advertising, product

7. To the extent that store image is associated with the attitude toward the private label merchandise sold by the store, we would expect a change in store to lead to brand switching. Unfortunately we know very little about private brand attitudes and how they are formed (Myers, 1967).

and service mix, type of store personnel, physical attributes, and clientele (Engel, Kollat, and Blackwell, 1968). To some extent each different store image will be associated with a slightly different kind of acceptable buying behavior, with respect to quality, price, style, product features and so forth. A second and perhaps more important consequence of the difference between stores, is the difference in the effectiveness of the salespeople that are encountered. In some stores the backgrounds and interests of the salespeople and the customer are more similar than in others that may be patronized. This becomes significant in the light of studies that show that the closer the similarity, the greater the probability of success by the salesman (Evans, 1963). Success here certainly includes overriding or changing the buyer's brand attitude.

Again, in measuring the effect of changing store environments we generally will not be able to get close to the actual behavior in the store. However, at a minimum, we can expect that the more stores a buyer patronizes the more likely we are to find that the facilitating aspects of the differences in environment lead to brand switching behavior.

Price and Financial Constraints

The economist's traditional concern with the effect of absolute price, in reducing funds available for other purchases, sheds little light on the effect of relative price differences between brands. This is not to say that the *absolute* price of the brand is not important, for it can determine whether the brand is seen as a good or bad value. However, it seems that the effect of price also depends on the accuracy of the prior knowledge of the price structure.

Appliance brand choice is probably subject to both these effects. Buyers first of all tend to confine their search to price levels that they can afford (Mueller, 1955, page 47), even though they have a high regard for other more expensive brands. Second, as the absolute price level increases, the normal search for information is intensified by people's feelings of financial stringency. Thus we

70

would expect that buyers in Criterion Group II, who purchased a brand they did not initially favor, would pay a lower than average price for the same type of appliance and would be subject to greater financial constraints. It does not follow that there would be any difference in income, in view of Parkinson's law that expenses invariably rise to meet (and possibly exceed) income, so that most income groups are not free to buy whatever they wish.

One complicating factor is the observed tendency for buyers to use price as an indicant of product quality (Tull et al., 1964). Also White (1966, page 92) argues that, "the quality–price ratio (getting the most quality for the lowest prices) does not work at all in product categories where the consumer finds her own self-worth elevated through the act of purchase." This means that, in product categories where it is very hard to evaluate the brands and the buyer has no previous experience, the above hypotheses may not hold. Then we have to treat high price as a favorable piece of information, and formulate our predictions in terms of exposure to information.

When a product is purchased on any kind of a regular basis we assume that the usual prices for all salient brands are known and have been internalized into the latent structure and the attitude. Thus if a brand is perceived as a poor value for the money it is not as well liked. However, short-term price "surprises" in the form of coupons, deals, combination packs, trading stamp allowances, and so forth are not liable to be internalized. The discovery that the price of a previously unfavored brand is temporarily the lowest of the product class, for example, will probably not cause any attitude change. But as Oxenfeldt et al. (1961) note, out attitudes toward money are of such great salience that the new low price cannot possibly be ignored. In such a case many buyers will not be able to justify paying a higher price. This tendency to switch to an un-favored brand because of price changes will become increasingly evident as the differences among brands diminish. Thus, we would expect, as we move from Criterion Group I to Group II, that the average unit price paid would decline, the range of prices paid for all brands would be broader, and the usage of coupons and deals would increase. This conclusion is consistent with several sets of empirical results, for example, "high deal-prone consumers exhibit less brand loyalty than those who are low deal-prone" (Webster, 1965, page 189) and, "Those loyal to a brand remain loyal; purchasing on deals tends to be concentrated among those with low brand loyalties" (Cunningham, 1956 page 117). Neither study was able to shed any light on the question of direction of causality between deal buying activity and brand loyalty. This suggests that we should also look at some independent constructs such as "loyalty-proneness" versus "economy consciousness" in contrasting the main criterion groups of the attitude–behavior model, even when the absolute price level of the product is not important.[8] However, the model would assign the cause of "disloyal" behavior to the environmental factors, in this case the effect of the deal on the price.

Family Decision Processes

Katz and Lazarsfeld make an important distinction between the *influences* on a buyer's attitude and *requests* which override the buyer's attitudes.

In the case of influences the decision-making power is solely in the hands of the wife—though she may take account of advice, testimonials, etc., just as she may give heed to friends, neighbors and others; in the case of requests, however, the decision-maker is, in effect, the one who makes the request (husband, or child, or other household member) and unless the wife dissents, she acts merely as a purchasing agent to carry the request into action.[9]

There are really three possible decision situations that are relevant to the model of attitudes and subsequent behavior. If the buyer's (usually the housewife's) attitudes prevail, there is no problem. In other cases where the buyer is interviewed, but is only carrying out the request of someone in the family, we might be seriously mislead. The solution is clear: Either interview the decision-maker, or delete

---

8. These variables will be discussed in greater detail later in this chapter.
9. Katz and Lazarsfeld (1955, page 245).

the household from the analysis. A final possibility is that the decision might be made after a compromise of all views or, at least, after considering the preferences of others. Coulson (1966, page 63) reports that most housewives *say* they take family brand preferences into account, when they know them. This proportion ranges from 73 per cent to 87 per cent of all housewives, depending on the visibility of the brand and the extent that it is changed before serving. Unfortunately we don't know whether there are likely to be differences of opinion among family members, and whether we can treat the resolution of the differences as an attitude change with the same effect as new information. The answer, no doubt, will vary between products, and depend on who in the household is regarded as the authority on the product.[10] To treat this variable as an environmental factor we can either contrast the two criterion groups according to the attitudes of other influential family members, or hope that the buyer's (usually the housewife's) attitude has internalized all the other points of view.

Moderating Effects

The development of a model of the brand attitude–brand choice behavior relationship has proceeded by first assuming isomorphism, and then hypothesizing various environmental influences which dampen the behavioral manifestation of attitudes. The relative influence of these environmental factors can be tested by contrasting the buyers whose behavior was inhibited with those whose behavior was facilitated.

For the test of the presence of environmental factors to be meaningful, the error of prediction should be reasonably small. That is, those people with the same initial brand attitude should have similar latent structures. We have already noted that this may

---

10. Much work is available on the general problem of joint family decision-making, but none directly applicable to brand choice (for useful reviews, see Kenkel, 1961; and Granbois, 1963).

not be the case—contrary to the classic psychometric theory underlying most scaling and testing work. This possibility has been partially confirmed as a result of some recent work designed to make aptitude tests better predictors, through an understanding of the causes of large errors of prediction (Ghiselli, 1963; and Tyler, 1965, page 141). The strategy has been to distinguish individuals with large absolute errors of prediction on a test from those with small errors, by various "moderators" which act as proxies for different psychological or latent structures. With this information it is possible to specify the cases in which the test score is appropriate for prediction. Thus if a test of occupational preferences, when compared to actual occupation, is a poor predictor for women but very good for men, subsequent use should be limited to men. We will follow this approach with one important difference. As described in Chapter 2, we will use the moderator variables that contribute the most to explaining the error of prediction as a basis for segmenting the sample. Then the attitude–behavior relationship will be re-evaluated for each segment, to determine the conditions under which brand attitudes are most useful as predictors of choice behavior.

No general principles about the nature of these moderator variables have been determined, although age and education often work (Ghiselli, 1963). Saunders has suggested various possibilities that provide some insight into the kind of processes to expect:

(a) Degree of "insight" may determine the degree of relationship between self-reports of personality and more objectively determined scores on the same traits. (b) Amount of "desire to make a good impression" may determine the relative efficacy of free-response and forced choice types of personality inventory. (c) Degree of "natural enthusiasm or ability to discover new interests" may determine the validity of interest measures for a variety of situations, even when "compulsiveness" is held constant. (d) Degree of "emotional stability" may determine the effectiveness of academic ability measures in predicting academic success.[11]

---

11. Saunders (1956, page 207). Saunders also provided (1956, page 210) a mathematical basis of moderated regression, as follows:

(a) The usual prediction situation is $Y = \bar{Y} + \sum_i a_i x_i \quad i:1 \ldots n.$

From this development it is easy to see that moderating effects act like interaction terms, as was suggested in Chapter 2.

Our task here is to specify moderator variables that will explain important differences in latent structures that are not already encompassed by attitude measures. One approach is to use variables that test theorists have found helpful, such as age and education. These, and other socioeconomic and demographic variables, serve as a good starting point. Such variables have always been useful to marketers because they are the basic means of directing marketing efforts to attractive groups of buyers. Unfortunately their overall contribution to explaining differences in brand choice behavior is usually modest at best. There are many alternatives to these basic variables; in fact at the extreme, almost every determinant of individual differences is probably relevant. We will take a middle course in this study, and confine our attention to variables that have had some success in similar contexts. In particular, the determinants of buying style, time pressure, attitude stability, and extraneous determinants of responses appear to have significant value.

Buying Style

Style is used here in the sense of relatively consistent modes of behavior across different buying situations. Our premise is that there will be differences in buyer's reactions even when they are confronted with the same purchasing environment, and to some extent this is a consequence of differences in buying style. The

---

(b) Substitute a linear function of the moderator z_i for the parameter a_i:

$$Y = \bar{Y} + \sum_i \left(\sum_j b_{ji} z_i \right) x_i$$

(c) Simplify to the general expression:

$$y = \bar{y} + \sum_i a_i x_i + \sum_i b_j z_j + \sum_{ij} c_{ij} x_i z_j$$

Once the cross-products $(x_i z_j)$ have been computed the equation can be fitted by any conventional regression technique.

range of possible styles is well illustrated by Wood's (1960, page 17) classification of buyers into six types:[12]

1. Habit-determined, brand loyal customers who tend to be satisfied with the last purchased product or brand.
2. Cognitive consumers who are sensitive to rational claims and are only conditionally brand loyal.
3. Price-cognitive consumers who decide principally on the basis of price or economy comparisons.
4. Impulse consumers who buy on the basis of physical appeal and are relatively insensitive to brand names.
5. "Emotional" reactors who tend to be responsive to what products symbolize and who are heavily swayed by "images."
6. New consumers not yet stabilized with respect to the psychological dimensions of consumer behavior.

Not all of these buying styles are independent, and some are more relevant to brand choice behavior than others. In fact, two more general dimensions of buying style appear to contain most of the important distinctions in the scheme used by Woods: namely, responsiveness to price changes and propensity to change. We will look at these two dimensions in detail, along with a third dimension, time pressure.

Responsiveness to price changes. Efforts to understand differences in buyer responses to price have largely dealt with the use of price as an indicant of quality or with the relationship of deal-proneness and brand loyalty. Other than this, very little is known about general characteristics that will tell us how the responses of individual buyers will vary when the (usually) inhibiting effects of price are removed. Several facets of this problem have recently been discussed by Lunn. His discussion is particularly useful because it indicates some of the issues that classification questions should address:

Firstly, there is what we call "Economy-mindedness"—the tendency to buy cheap rather than expensive goods, to keep within a strict house-keeping

---

12. We have followed the discussion of Myers and Reynolds (1967, page 102) here. Also in this source is a discussion of the few studies that bear on the validity of Wood's attempt at classification (see pages 103–107 inclusive).

limit; to deny oneself luxuries. This is quite different from what we call "Bargain-Seeking," which reflects the satisfaction of saving a few pennies by shopping carefully and comparing prices, and the relish of hunting for bargains.[13]

In general we would expect individual differences along the "Bargain-Seeking" dimension to account for most of the variability in response to price changes, deals, coupons, and so forth. In that sense it serves as a significant moderating effect.

Propensity to change. This broad term seems to summarize many disparate attempts to explain an individual's willingness to change an ongoing pattern of behavior. Relevant research and theorizing seems to encompass impulsiveness, willingness to experiment, innovativeness, persuasibility, and so forth. We will examine each of these areas in turn.

1. Impulsiveness. A useful analytic definition of impulse purchasing has been suggested by Willett and Kollatt:

> Impulse buying may differ from planned buying in that fewer evaluative criteria may be employed, the time spent in evaluation may be compressed, and the role structure involved in evaluation may be unique. Impulse purchasing may enable the consumer to perform a more comprehensive and intensive evaluation of competing solutions; that is, by postponing this activity until he is in the store he may be better able to compare prices, quality and the availability of substitutes and complements.[14]

It is not the fact that purchases may be planned or unplanned that is the concern here. Rather, it is the likelihood that the buyer may reevaluate the alternatives (and perhaps crystallize previously unverbalized cognitions), and be open to new possibilities. To the extent that a buyer is more or less prone to make these on-the-spot reevaluations we would expect more or less rigidity in response to environmental factors. Unfortunately, impulsiveness is thought to be a complex variable of itself, depending on perceived needs, personality, and competence in problem solving. Because of this underlying complexity a measure of self-perceived impulsiveness might serve to indicate this moderator.

---

13. Lunn (1966, page 167).
14. 1964, page 217.

2. "A change is refreshing"—Howard and Sheth (1966, page 2-50) suggest that exploratory behavior, including the search for new information and new alternatives, is partially explainable by the role of ambiguity from various sources, "Berlyne (1963) has suggested that there is a certain intermediate level of ambiguity which the buyer tolerates and accepts as satisfactory . . . if ambiguity goes below the intermediate level, the buyer finds it too simple (too routine or too monotonous) a situation and deliberately tries to inject ambiguity . . . by seeking new alternatives and new information." This concept is clearly only relevant to regularly purchased items, and may vary as a moderator according to past experience, an individual's tolerance for ambiguity, and so forth. For an empirical test it might be sufficient to use actual usage as the moderator—at least until there is more evidence on the existence of this kind of behavior in the buying context.

3. Some aspects of the work on the characteristics of innovators (Rogers, 1963) and the personality correlates of persuasibility (Hovland et al., 1953) clearly encompass the specific problem of forecasting propensity or desire to change. However it is doubtful that this work can be immediately applied to brand choice behavior in a stable market.

Most research on innovativeness uses the time of acceptance of a significant innovation as the dependent variable and proceeds to search for plausible covarying (although not necessarily causal) variables. The first obstacle to the use of this research is that the risk entailed in trying a major innovation, is far greater than in switching to another brand in the same product class. Second, many of the best covarying variables are merely descriptions of the characteristic we are trying to describe. For example, Rogers and Stanfield (1966) have found that "attitude toward change" is the most widely used indicant of innovativeness.[15] Lastly, the decision

---

15. Rogers and Stanfield (1966) review several other less used indicants, with better predictive power, such as knowledgeability and aspirations for children. In addition, a number of demographic variables were shown to relate closely to innovativeness. However they all have the disadvantage of being more relevant to product decisions than to brand decisions.

to switch brands is not likely to be made much in advance of the actual purchase, whereas the adoption process apparently passes through a number of stages stretched over a considerable period of time.

We seem to move closer to what we are looking for in the research on personality correlates of persuasibility. If people vary in the ease with which they can be convinced of anything, then it should follow that there will be corresponding variations (1) in the acceptance of competitive communications, and (2) in willingness to try other brands. This logic is probably correct—judging from the number of people who have tried to verify it. But thus far the practical results have been very unsatisfactory. The problems are many, beginning with the original work concerned with identifying relevant characteristics. Among the many personality measures tried, only self-esteem has shown a moderately consistent relationship to persuasibility. An immediate drawback to the use of self-esteem as a moderator is the dependence on various aspects of the communications situation. Further, as Cox and Bauer (1964) have shown, the relationship is often curvilinear. A review of these difficulties led Carey (1963, page 37) to conclude, ". . . that, at the present time at least, the work has little relevance for marketing." Our present feeling is that the gains from using personality measures are likely to be small in the face of the measurement problems and the difficulties of properly interpreting the results. Furthermore, in view of the recent "bad press" of applications of the personality concept to marketing problems (for instance, Yoell, 1966), the prospects for future applications are limited.

Time pressure. We have included time pressure under the rubric of buying style, primarily because lack of time may preclude certain styles of buying. Certainly any propensity to change may be negated if time is very short. Under these circumstances only the most familiar alternatives are liable to be considered or even perceived. Thus, in a more general sense, time pressure also acts as a moderator, because it will adversely affect the perception of, or search for, new information.

79

Attitude Stability

Our confidence in the predictive power of a person's attitude declines at approximately the same rate as the respondent's uncertainty about her response increases and interest in the attitude object declines. At the point where the answer is primarily a guess, triggered by some forgotten and probably irrelevant association or by a desire to please or get rid of an interviewer, a correct prediction is purely fortuitous. Under these circumstances, behavior is entirely determined by the environment at the time of decision. Clearly, then, the two determinants of attitude stability will have a significant moderating effect.[16] Although confidence and involvement are likely to be closely associated, they do have different characteristics and implications for attitude research, so we will look at them separately.

Involvement was previously defined as the general level of interest in the object, or the centrality of the object to the respondent's ego. There is a strong intuitive appeal to the notion that level of involvement is closely related to the polarity of the attitude, or the amount of affect toward object. Peak (1955) appears to have been the first to question this notion of a direct relation. At the moment the tendency among attitude theorists is to argue that involvement and polarity are more likely to be independent (Feldman, 1966).

Most of the empirical research has supported the intuitive relation of involvement (usually called intensity or strength of feeling in the research reports) and polarity. If the two variables are measured independently, and then plotted, the result is usually a U-shaped or J-shaped curve (see Guttman and Suchman, 1947, and McCroskey *et al.*, 1967). However, the strength of the relation seems to be influenced by the way the involvement or intensity question is asked. Thus Weksel and Hennes (1965) found low correlations (r^2 of 0.10 to 0.35) with semantic differential scales

---

16. A third influence on attitude stability is changes in the mood or state of mind of the respondent. Since this kind of change is brought about by internal pressure, irrespective of the stability of the attitude, it is better considered as one of the extraneous determinants in the next section.

and such questions as "How strongly do you hold this particular view?" and "How sure are you of the rating you have just made?" The latter question deals with confidence or cognitive certainty, a concept we will look at shortly.

A good deal is known about the effects of different levels of involvement. Not surprisingly, "Those who lack interest in the topic are likely to give perfunctory responses, (in which) a 'yes' or 'no' answer is almost a matter of choice" (Kendall, 1954, page 108). Disinterest also contaminates the response to persuasive communications. In the absence of internal standards for assessing a communication (or an attitude scale) the respondent may be more influenced by the prestige, and so forth, of the communicator or researcher, the order of the arguments, the kind of presentation, and the type of content, (Sherif, Sherif, and Nebergall, 1965, page 181). Underlying both these effects, and many similar effects, is a general tendency for the probability of attitude change to vary inversely with the level of involvement. The specific roles that involvement plays have been well summarized by Engel and Light (1968): (1) Attitudes are easier to change when the existing mass of stored information is small. (2) Attitudes having centrality are the most resistant to change. "This is a function of the extent to which the object is intimately related to the self-concept, important values or motives." (3) "Attitudes that are highly interconnected with others resist change. Human beings strive, of course, to retain balance in an attitude system, and change in one generally leads to change in another." Lastly, the Sherifs (1965) have shown that as involvement increases, there is a greater likelihood that discrepant communications will be perceived as being farther away from a person's attitude than they are in reality.[17] As a consequence attitude change becomes less likely.

Studies of involvement in marketing contexts have largely focused on differences between products. For example, Bogart

---

17. This is known as a contrast effect. The opposite is the assimilation effect. In the last five years an impressive amount of research has supported this effect, for example Eagly (1967), Freedman (1964), and Zimbardo (1960).

(1967, page 204 *et seq*.) reports a study in which involvement with the product was a function of (1) the degree to which the consumer found the product pleasant, or pleasant to use, (2) the degree of interest in reading and hearing about new developments in the product field, and (3) willingness to talk about the product. The variability in "high involvement" scores was striking. For example, with women the extent of high involvement varied from 66 per cent for canned vegetables to seven per cent for vodka. From this, and other studies, Bogart has developed some basic propositions about product interest:

1. An expensive item is more likely to arouse the consumer's emotional involvement. . . .
2. A product about which the consumer feels deeply is most likely to arouse an active, purposeful search for information when he is in the market.
3. A product category in which the customer perceives brands as being very different creates a more purposeful selective interest in advertising.
4. Most products . . . arouse comparatively little involvement. They are likely to be inexpensive and they demand rather effortless or routine decision making.[18]

However, Bogart also warns that high product involvement may not necessarily lead to a strong interest in the differences among brands.[19] Yet it is this kind of specific involvement that is likely to result in a moderating effect on predictions of brand choice behavior. This consideration, coupled with Kendall's (1954) finding that involvement can best be gauged by simply asking the respondents to classify themselves, suggests that involvement be measured by direct questioning regarding interest in the differences among brands in the product class in which brand attitude measures are collected.[20] Kendall also suggests that, under some circum-

---

18. Bogart (1967, page 203).

19. He cites the finding that "9 out of 10 men and 8 out of 10 women considered bread extremely pleasant to use, but only about 1 in 3 people liked to talk about bread and only half thought that there were important differences among brands of bread" (page 206).

20. This direct approach has the further virtue of avoiding the difficult problem of distinguishing true change, from change due to instability, when the alternative measurement strategy of repeat interviews is employed (as suggested by Clover, 1950).

stances, the interest of the respondent could be categorized on the basis of manifested interest. This encompasses, "behavior patterns, such as being regarded as a source of authority or an opinion leader, or spontaneous mention of a topic in answer to an open-ended question" (page 106).

Relatively less is known about the effect that the level of *confidence* in attitude judgments has on the stability of brand judgments. When we look at some of the reasons that confidence may vary it is obvious that the moderating effect is likely to be considerable. First, confidence in brand judgments is likely to mirror the level of involvement in differences among brands; if for no other reason than a person who lacks interest will not likely have the information or experience necessary to make a confident judgment. Beyond this, the confidence level may also reflect uncertainty about the correctness of the brand judgment, or ambiguity as to the meaning of the attitude object (Zajonc and Morrisett, 1960). Both these conditions can be present even when involvement is strong, and will directly influence the stability of the attitude. For example, if a respondent is unable to make any distinction between adjacent attitude statements or categories, the ensuing uncertainty is liable to lead to a random choice, vacillation, an insistence on giving a qualified answer or refusal to answer. The response is sure to be highly unstable.

Extraneous Determinants of Response

A distressing number of these determinants have been identified. To the extent that they are present in any attitude measurement situation we are unable to, "interpret . . . responses as reflecting the particular variable of concern," (Scott, 1966). These determinants may be either random, due to errors and carelessness, or systematic, in which case they affect all responses in a similar way. According to Scott, the *systematic* determinants most likely to be present in measurement situations are the tendency to reply in a "socially desirable way and the tendency to acquiesce or give only favorable responses." Of the two confounding tendencies, the most serious is the acquiescence set or yea-saying response style, since there is then the possibility that similar latent structures will not be classified as similar if some respondents have an automatic favorable response bias. Also, for brand attitudes, there are generally fewer opportunities to make a favorable impression with the interviewer by responding in a socially desirable way (although this problem is potentially serious with products such as cosmetics, where the buyer's self-esteem and the prestige of the product are important influences).

What appears as an acquiescence set is actually a compound of two influences. First, there is a strong tendency for this kind of response bias among people who can be described as impulsively over-expressive; they are, "individuals with weak ego controls, who accept impulses without reservation and who 'agree' and easily respond to stimuli exerted on them" (Couch and Keniston, 1960). These tendencies really take root, "when the rater does not feel strongly one way or the other; when he is unfamiliar with the object being rated; when the best information he can bring to bear is fragmentary, vague and half-forgotten . . . "(Wells, 1964). This reinforces the moderating effect of attitude instability on the attitude–behavior relationship. Not only does it make buyers overreact to environmental influences, but it also tends to misclassify them accordingly to the initial attitude.

Wells (1964) presents data on brand attitudes by groups of yea-sayers and nay-sayers. The group ratings differed by average scores of one to nine per cent of the length of the scale, depending on the popularity of the brand and the product. These average figures conceal a great deal of individual variability; but even so the contribution to error in the attitude–behavior relationship is considerable. Wells has also found that the yea-sayers claim to buy more products than nay-sayers do, and to some extent actually do buy more. Apparently then these groups also differ in overt behavior.

The analysis design described in this chapter makes it possible to determine objectively the influence of acquiescence set on the observed relationship, if an acquiescence score can be determined for each buyer. Such a score is surprisingly elusive, even when batteries of special scales are administered or clinical tests and social influence experiments are directed toward this end. Furthermore, different approaches often give contradictory results (see Moscovici, 1963, page 237). Since none of these tools are generally feasible in field studies of brand attitudes, other less direct approaches must be taken. One possibility is to compare criterion groups according to their average attitude over the major brands in a variety of product classes. A consistently favorable attitude toward all brands would be evidence of an acquiescence set. Another more speculative possibility is a measure of the consistency in the judgments toward various attributes of the brand itself. These two possibilities have been related in research, reported by Moscovici (1963, page 238), which shows that as an attitude becomes less structured and less definite it is more likely to be stated as a favorable attitude. Specifically, "A favorable attitude is, in a way, an open vacant attitude, and thereby less definite. An unfavorable attitude is both more closed and more clearly structured." This suggests that lack of stability in an attitude may lead to more variable judgments of the various attributes of the brand *and* to a general upward bias in the attitude.[21]

Conclusions

With this chapter we have completed the development of a model of the relationship of brand attitudes and brand choice behavior. The model confirms the general impression that the prediction of behavior solely from initial attitudes is clouded by many interacting influences. Fortunately the model provides a means of classifying, and sometimes understanding, many of the various influences. So far as classification is concerned the model

---

21. Moscovici (1963) cites the finding of Gage and Chatterjee (1960), that negative items are more valid than positive items, in support of this hypothesis.

requires a distinction between environmental factors, which determine the *form* of the relationship, and moderating effects, which lead to unpredictable variability in the buyer's response to the environment and reduce the predictive *strength* of the relationship. Our understanding of the environmental factors is more complete, as the direction of their influence is almost always to dampen the behavioral manifestation of the latent structure. With the moderating effects however there is no certainty as to the direction of influence, although there will certainly be some damping effects in addition to the error inducing effects.

In general we cannot say which influences will have the greatest impact on the relationship. This becomes a matter for empirical testing. Eventually, if the model is tested in enough buying contexts the results would permit some generalizations about the relative importance of the different influences. Such a venture is fraught with problems, including the scarcity of appropriate panel data and of variables that both reflect the properties of the postulated influences and are roughly comparable in different product categories. This latter problem becomes an issue in Chapter 5, when we test for the presence of environmental factors and moderating effects in purchases of appliances in one case, and a regularly purchased food product in another. Before we can do this we have to define various criterion groups which may be differentially influenced, and this requires that we know the nature of the attitude–behavior relationship. This is the concern of the next chapter.

Chapter 4

Some Empirical Results: The Relationship of Attitude and Brand Choice Behavior

This chapter provides an empirical complement to the theoretical discussion of the attitude–behavior relationship in the second chapter. Two sets of data will be used to test the model described in the earlier chapter. Both are panel studies of purchase behavior, in which brand attitudes were elicited at the beginning of the panel and actual purchases were recorded for five to six months. Thus they both meet the minimum standard for satisfactory measures established in Chapter 1; that is, over-time comparisons of attitudes with behavior on the individual level. First we will briefly review the nature of the data in order to understand some of the limitations that are necessarily placed on the testing process. The major limitation is that one panel is for durable goods, with medium to long repurchase cycles, which precludes obtaining probability measures of purchasing. With this panel only the aggregate test of the relationship, described in Chapter 2, is applicable. The second panel deals with a rapid turnover convenience food product where purchase probabilities can be estimated fairly reliably. Both aggregate and individual level tests are applicable for this data, with the further advantage that the shape of the attitude–behavior relationship can also be estimated for one brand. Because the aggregate relationship will be examined for both panels, the chapter will include a comparison of the two different kinds of purchase behavior.

Description of the Purchase Panels

THE DURABLES PANEL

This panel consists of two personal interviews, separated by six months, of 150 households. The first interview collected a wide range of household background data on demographic characteristics, media and shopping habits, appliance inventory (in 27 major, electronic, and houseware product categories), appliance purchasing intentions, and attitudes toward seven nationally distributed, full-line brands of appliances. The second interview concentrated on appliance purchasing and repair experiences in the previous six months, as well as any changes in household characteristics (moves, salary increases, children, and so on), and brand attitudes and purchasing intentions.

The durables panel was designed and implemented by the General Electric Company as part of the pilot test of a proposed consumer information system. Because of the small sample size the findings from this panel are decidely exploratory. Nonetheless, the panel members did acquire 186 appliances, in addition to gifts received from outside sources. Because the seven brands given attitude ratings are only part of the appliance market, which includes up to 150 brands in one or more product categories, only 70 of these acquisitions could be included in the analysis of this chapter. These acquisitions were made by 49 households. By limiting the analysis to an overall, "composite" brand, as well as the two largest brands, it is possible to obtain results that are quite meaningful and capable of comparison with those of the non-durables panel. Also, by concentrating on composite and large brands we ensure that the market meets the stability requirement.

Other details about the panel necessary to understanding the results and potential biases will be introduced as required, or can be found in Appendix B. The construction of an equal interval attitude scale for appliance brand attitudes is discussed in Appendix D.

NON-DURABLES PANEL

These data were collected as part of the Columbia University Research Project on Buyer Behavior. The overall design of this project used two matched mail diary panels to follow the progress of a new brand of food product, for five months following test market introduction. Both panels were selected from the same test market area. One panel was only asked to make bi-weekly reports of purchases in five separate food product categories. The second panel was further asked to complete a lengthy mail questionnaire at the beginning of the panel, and was telephoned twice during the panel period and once at the end. The additional data obtained in the mail and telephone questionnaires included (1) basic classi-fication data on innovativeness, media and shopping habits, price consciousness, perceived time pressure, eating habits, and other dimensions relevant to the product categories under study, (2) baseline attitudes, images, and intentions for the major brand in three different product categories, (3) changes in awareness and attitude toward the newly introduced brand, as well as toward existing brands in the immediate product category, as the panel progressed, and (4) changes in exposure to personal and imper-sonal sources of information about the new brand, and the com-peting brands. The other, "control" panel was used to measure the sensitizing effects of the questioning during the panel. Details about the characteristics of the households in the panel, means of recruit-ment, types of incentives, and possible response biases are discussed in Appendix C.

While the overall project was primarily interested in the product category in which the new brand was being introduced, full data on attitudes and behavior were collected for the largest selling brand in two other moderately similar product categories. In part this served to disguise the basic intent, but there was also a (subsequently unfounded) possibility that the three product categories were directly competing for the same business.[1] One of these "other" product categories is very appropriate for the testing of the attitude–behavior relationship. First, the market for this product was very stable during the period of the test, that is, no new products were launched, nor were there major promotional changes. Second, this is a product where the housewife is almost invariably one of the users. This is important, as the housewife was the source of the attitude rating and the purchase reports. Third, both the brand chosen for study and the major competing brand, which are about the same size, are reported to have between 90 and 95 per cent all-commodity distribution in food stores. Finally, the typical purchase cycle is about two weeks, which means that on average there were eleven distinct brand choice decisions on which to base a purchase probability measure.

Although the panel started with 1100 households, only 955 completed the mail questionnaire which provided the semantic differential scales of attitude toward the brand under study. The equal interval properties of these scales, and the procedure for determining the dimensionality of the brand attitude, are discussed in Appendix D. Subsequent panel attrition reduced the number of eligible buyers of the product class to 238 (of which 18 were not aware of the brand or were aware but did not have an initial attitude). This group provides the basic sample for the forthcoming tests of the non-durables attitude–behavior relationship. Details about the nature of this sample, and the procedure by which it was chosen, are also to be found in Appendix C. Before turning to the aggregate test of the relationship with the two sets of data, it should be noted that a basic distinction[2] is drawn between

---

1. This possibility was tested directly by asking each respondent: "Would you say that *product A* and *product B* are very similar, quite similar, somewhat similar or not similar at all?" and repeating for the product pairs AC and BC. Only 15 of the 220 buyers of product A, which we are interested in, also bought products B and C, and regarded A as very similar to B and C. Even if we assume that "very similar" means "I'd substitute these products readily," the amount of substitution is negligible.

2. The cut-off point between heavy and light usage was based on an analysis of usage patterns for the product.

heavy and light buyers (more than or less than ten units) of the non-durables product category throughout this chapter. There is ample evidence that heavy buyers are strategically more important (Twedt, 1964, page 71), and behave quite differently (Ehrenberg, 1964; and Farley and Kuehn, 1965). In this instance 54 per cent of the 170 buyers of the brand were classified as heavy users of the product.

An Aggregative Test of the Relationship

In Chapter 2 it was suggested that the initial attitudes of groups of buyers and non-buyers of the brand could be contrasted, as an initial approximation to determining the presence of a relationship. We would expect that the proportion of buyers of the brand per attitude category would increase as the attitude becomes more favorable. We will look at durables and non-durables separately, and then contrast these two products to determine the influence of length of purchase cycle on the attitude–behavior relationship.

The Durables Case

Attitude scores for each of seven major brands were obtained for each household. These scores have a range of 0 to 7.5 on an equal-appearing interval scale (see Appendix D). In Table 4–1 we have classified buyers according to their attitude toward the brand they purchased without distinguishing among brands. Thus the "buyer" column is based on 70 purchases and their associated attitude ratings. If we remove these ratings from the total of 150 households times seven ratings per household, which equals 1050 ratings, we have a distribution of the attitudes towards all the brands that were not purchased. This is equivalent to the ratings of the "non-buyers" of a composite brand.

A chi-square test showed the two overall distributions to be significantly different. To determine just where the significant differences lay, the overall chi-square was partitioned into additive components, using a procedure outlined by Maxwell (1961, Chapter 3). The components of chi-square have the following significance in the relationship:

Component of χ^2 due to:	χ^2	Degrees of Freedom	Significance Level
1. Difference between two favorable groups and remaining groups	7.59	1	$P < 0.005$
2. Differences within two favorable groups	4.90	1	$P < 0.025$
3. Differences within remaining groups	0.21	3	Not significant
Total or overall chi-square	12.70	5	$P < 0.025$

From the partitioning we see that the results of the overall test are largely due to buyers having favorable attitudes, and non-buyers having neutral or unfavorable attitudes. There is no serious confounding effect due to the large observable buyer versus non-buyer difference within the favorable group.

The relationship observed in Table 4–1, obscures several important factors by aggregating across different categories of appliances and seven brands. If we take the price of the appliance as a rough indicant of the importance of the purchase, it appears that brand attitudes are only useful predictors of brand choice for the less important low-priced appliances. This is consistent with the prediction that environmental factors become progressively more influential as the importance of the purchase increases. With high-priced products initial brand attitudes may be irrelevant. In

Table 4–1—Distribution of Attitudes of Buyers and Non-Buyers of a "Composite" Appliance Brand
(Percentage of Group in Each Attitude Category)

Attitude Category (and Range)		Buyers	Non-Buyers
1. Extremely favorable	(0 to 0.4)	31.5%	11.8%
2. Favorable	(0.5 to 1.9)	26.0	26.6
3. Neutral	(2.0 to 3.4)	27.0	28.6
4. Unfavorable	(3.5 to 5.9)	15.5	20.5
5. Extremely unfavorable	(6.0 to 7.5)	—	4.7
6. Don't know or No answer		— ⊙	7.6
TOTAL		100%	100%

Table 4–2, $75.00 was arbitrarily selected as the dividing line between high and low-priced appliances. Items just under this dividing line quite likely assumed considerable importance to the purchaser; but in these cases we cannot be as certain that they justified the extensive search and price comparison activity usually associated with the purchase of a stove, refrigerator, or washing machine, for example.

Individual brands also exhibit markedly different types of attitude–behavior relationships within the general pattern. For example, Figures 4–1 and 4–2 contrast the cumulative proportions of groups holding an attitude toward one of two large selling brands according to whether they bought that brand, some other brand, or made no appliance acquisitions. Attitudes are useful predictors in the case of Brand A, where the tenor of initial opinions is not very enthusiastic. However they contribute little information to distinguish buyers of Brand B from non-buyers, because the initial opinions are almost entirely favorable. Of course, at the individual brand level there is always the danger that the items used to make up the attitude scale will not encompass some feature that is particularly salient to one brand. For example, the uniformly favorable attitudes toward Brand B indicate that most people are aware of that brand, would recommend it to their friends, have confidence in the quality of construction, and believe that maintenance is readily obtainable. (These items are described in detail in Appendix D.) If however, most purchase decisions were influenced by the price of Brand B relative to other brands, the availability of installment credit, or by specific design features, the attitude scores used to construct Figure 4–2 might not be relevant.

Table 4–2—Distribution of Brand Attitudes for Purchases of High and Low-Priced Appliances
(Proportion of Group in Each Attitude Category)

Attitude Category (and Range)		Purchase Was High-Priced	Purchase Was Low-Priced
Extremely Favorable or Favorable	(0 to 1.9)	6 (33.3%)	33 (63.5%)
Neutral or Unfavorable	(2.0 to 5.9)	12 (66.6%)	19 (36.5%)
Total purchases		18 (100%)	52 (100%)

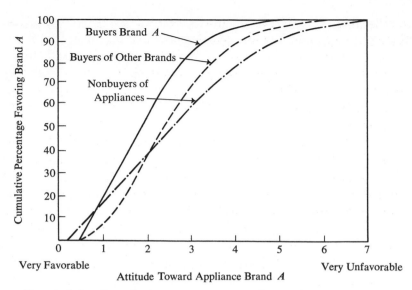

Figure 4–1. Cumulative proportions within attitude categories favoring appliance brand A

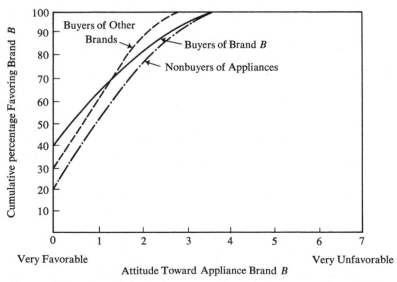

Figure 4–2. Cumulative proportions within attitude categories favoring appliance brand B.

But, because the attitude measures work well in general this is not likely to be a significant problem.

The Non-Durables Case

The attitude measure used in this aggregate test is a seven-point semantic differential scale designed to measure general "affect," toward the "analysis"[3] brand. One pole of the scale read, "In general I like it [the brand]," while the other pole read, "In general I don't like it." This can be assumed to be an equal interval scale equivalent to the one used for the appliance brands. Because this scale meets the standards for an attitude measure laid out in Chapter 2, it will also be used for the subsequent individual level tests of the attitude–behavior relationship.

Two types of non-buyers of the analysis brand must be distinguished: those who bought the product but didn't buy the analysis brand, and non-buyers of the product itself. Because we are interested in brand choice and not product choice, the first type is more relevant. This will be the definition used in comparing the durables and non-durables situation, and in determining the significance of the relationship. However both classes of non-buyers are shown in Table 4–3.

Table 4–3—Distribution of Attitudes of Buyers and Non-Buyers of a Non-Durable Analysis Brand
(Percentage of Group in Each Attitude Category)

	Buyers of Analysis Brand (n=170)	Non-Buyers of Analysis Brand (n=50)	Non-Buyers of Product (n=644)
1. Very Favorable	39.5%	13.2%	12.6%
2. Quite favorable	15.8	3.2	4.3
3. Favorable	11.3	6.6	5.1
4. Neutral	19.7	37.4	21.8
5. Unfavorable	3.4	5.0	5.2
6. Quite unfavorable	2.3	6.0	6.9
7. Very unfavorable	4.0	18.0	19.4
Don't Know/No Answer	4.0	10.0	24.4
Total	100%	100%	100%

3. Throughout this discussion the name of the analysis brand, the competing brands, and the product class will be disguised.

By inspection it is apparent that the buyers of the analysis brand are sharply distinguishable by the favorableness of their attitude, and their ability to form an attitude in the first place. Once again we can partition the attitudes into those who are favorable (categories 1, 2, and 3) versus all others, to determine which differences are most significant within the overall relationship:

Component of χ^2 due to:	χ^2	Degrees of Freedom	Significance Level
1. Difference between favorable groups $(1+2+3)$ and all others	38.50	1	$P < 0.001$
2. Differences within the favorable group	3.88	2	not significant
3. Differences within the remainder	15.51	4	$P < 0.001$
Total or overall chi-square	57.89	7	$P < 0.001$

As in the durables case, the partitioning reveals that the strong observed relationship is largely attributable to buyers of the analysis brand having favorable attitudes, and non-buyers (who did make purchases in the product class) having neutral or unfavorable attitudes.

The buyer classification used here is inflated by 78 light buyers of the product category. If this group is contrasted with the heavy buyers we see that their lack of interest in the product is reflected in luke-warm attitudes toward the "analysis" brand. This point is best made by reference to Figure 4–3, where the proportions in each attitude category, for several groups of buyers and non-buyers, are cumulated starting with the most favorable category. Not only does this indicate a strong relationship between attitude and behavior by the criteria for an aggregate test, it also means that this brand has been successful in satisfying the needs of the critical heavy buyer group. Had the spread between the attitudes of heavy and light buyers been narrower it would have suggested that the brand is not successful in converting light users and probably is having difficulty maintaining a stable "loyal" core of heavy buyers. The only way this possibility could be confirmed is with a test of the individual relationships. Before we turn to this test let us summarize the results to this point in terms of inter-product differences.

Inter-Product Differences

To establish comparability between durables and non-durables we have (1) given both attitude scales the same range of values, (2) limited the comparison to buyers of the brand (the "composite" durables brand and the "analysis" non-durables brand) versus non-buyers of the brand who do make purchases in the product category, and (3) measured the strength of the relationship by subtracting the proportion of all non-buyers in each attitude category from the proportion of buyers. Note that the area bounded by the resulting curve above the line 0–0 in Figure 4–4, is theoretically the same as the area below the line 0–0.

The important implication of Figure 4–4 is that attitudes are better discriminators better buyers and non-buyers for a product with a short cycle; consequently, as the cycle shortens the

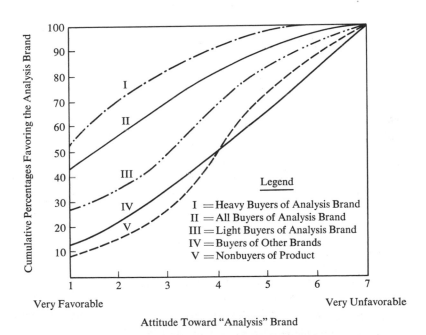

Figure 4–3. Cumulative proportions within attitude categories for a Non-Durables Analysis Brand.

damping influence of the environmental factors diminishes. The latter statement makes more sense when we consider that the extreme effect of the environmental factors is to eliminate the predictive value of attitudes. At this extreme, the distance between buyers and non-buyers is negligible, and the curve of Figure 4–4 would be horizontal. Because of the pronounced relationship for durables we can conclude that this null effect will not be encountered as long as there is some differentiation among brands.

An Individual Level Test of the Relationship

This discussion will be limited to the non-durables panel data, for it is only here that we can generate a probability measure of choice behavior. This behavior measure will first be linked with the seven-point semantic differential attitude scale, in the context of the model developed in Chapter 2. This will be the key test of

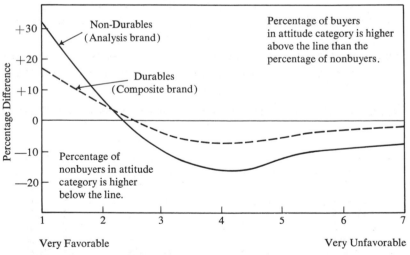

Figure 4–4. The difference between attitudes of buyers and non-buyers: Durables and non-durables

that model. Later in this chapter we will examine differences in the behavior of heavy and light buyers, and test two underlying assumptions of the model (1) that the predictive power of a uni-dimensional measure of affect will not be improved by additional brand attitude components (dimensions) or intentions to purchase, and (2) that probability of brand choice is the most relevant measure of behavior in this product category.

Testing the Attitude–Behavior Model

A description of the attitude measure can be found earlier in this chapter (see Table 4–3) and in Appendix D. The brand choice measure was constructed, for each household, by summing the total number of brand choice *decisions* and dividing this number into the number of decisions to buy the "analysis" brand, which is under study here. In other words we obtain the proportion of the total number of decisions, in favor of the analysis brand during the five month duration of the panel. When a household reported purchasing two brands of the same product on the same day, or bought one brand at two different stores on the same day, the rule was to count this as two brand decisions. Fortunately this kind of behavior was not prevalent. Some of the characteristics of this behavior measure can be seen from Table 4–4. Recall that light buyers are those who bought less than ten units in five months.

Table 4–4—Probability of Choice of "Analysis" Brand—Non-Durables Panel Data

(Percentage of column total in brackets)

Probability of Purchase	Heavy Buyers	Light Buyers	Total Buyers of Product*
1.00	24 (21.4%)	40 (31.8%)	64 (26.9%)
0.80 – 0.99	13 (11.6)	0 (0)	13 (5.5)
0.60 – 0.79	18 (16.1)	11 (8.7)	29 (12.2)
0.40 – 0.59	19 (17.0)	23 (18.2)	42 (17.6)
0.20 – 0.39	11 (9.8)	7 (5.5)	18 (7.6)
0.01 – 0.19	8 (7.1)	1 (0.8)	9 (3.8)
0.0	19 (17.0)	44 (35.0)	63 (26.5)
	112	126	238

* Includes 18 buyers without an initial attitude

99

Heavy buyers purchased from 10 to 95 units in this same period. The two noteworthy features of Table 4–4 are the pronounced tendencies toward the two extremes of complete loyalty and non-buying, which lead to a sway-backed distribution; and the bunching of the distribution of probabilities for light buyers at the ends and the middle.[4] This last effect is caused by the inefficiency of estimates based on a small total number of decisions. The question is whether or not this has any influence on the relationship of attitudes and behavior.

First, however, we will test the model across all buyers of the product, as the model is formulated in these terms. Since testing implies determining both the *strength* and the *shape* of the relationship (the latter is necessary to check for possible non-monotonicity), least-squares polynomials of the following form[5] were computed:

$$Y = \alpha + B_1 X + B_2 X^2 + \cdots + B_6 X^6 \text{ (6th degree maximum).}$$

The dependent variable is probability of brand choice $(P\{K|P_i\})$ and the independent variable is initial attitude (A_i).[6] Logarithmic transformations of the independent variable were also attempted, but did not improve the strength of the relationship.

So far as *strength* of the relationship is concerned the *linear* term has a simple correlation coefficient of -0.492 with an $F(1,218) = 71.35$ which is significant at $P < 0.001$. If we keep fitting succes-

---

4. Both of these features may also be attributable to the fact that this probability has some of the undesirable features of percentages. "Percentage data follow the binomial distribution and their variances are correlated with the sample results. . . . However percentages can be converted via the arcsin transformation to normally distributed data" (Banks, 1965, page 202). This transformation has not been attempted here, because similar models have not done so, and the conversion to a range of $0°$ to $90°$ would confuse interpretation. At the same time Frank (1966, page 253) notes that the variance of brand loyalty measures is sometimes stabilized by either the arcsin transform, or the double-log transform.

5. This program is part of the BMD package of programs. See Dixon (1964, page 297).

6. All subsequent calculations are based on the 220 households that expressed an attitude. The 18 that were blank were dropped because there was no way to estimate an attitude score. For example, eight of the blanks were initially unaware of the brand under study.

sively higher order equations we find that, according to the sum of squares accounted for by each additional term, there is little point to pushing further than a linear term (see Table 4–5). Taking these results at face value there is not much to get excited about. We have shown that there is a highly significant relationship, but we are not able to absorb a great deal of the response variability. Nonetheless, the predictive performance of the attitude scale was much better than the r^2 of 0.09 for a measure of *prior usage* of the brand. This variable asked whether the buyer had used the brand before the study and, if so, how recently the brand had been used. Those buyers who said they had not purchased the brand before the study had an average brand choice probability of 0.43. This figure is difficult to interpret because some of this group were probably new to the product class. By comparison, those who had bought the brand in the month just before the study began had an average brand choice probability of 0.69.

On a relative basis, we can say that attitudes alone are as good as other possible predictors, and in many cases, better. That is, no matter what approach we take to predicting brand choice behavior, there is a large, and seemingly irreducible amount of variability. (In fact, no matter what dependent variable is used—whether usage, media exposure, or even the determinants of attitudes—and how many independent variables are incorporated, it is seldom that R^2 of more than 0.20 to 0.30 are obtained in buyer behavior research.[7] This is not surprising, given the large

Table 4–5—Sum of Squares Associated with Polynomial Terms Describing the Attitude-Behavior Relationship

(Percentage of total sum of squares)

Linear	Quadratic	Cubic	Quartic	Quintic	Sextic	Sum of All Terms
24.2%	—	1.4%	—	0.3%	1.6%	27.7%

7. For recent examples of the low levels of predictions obtained at the individual level see Wilson (1966), Pessemier and Tigert(1966) and Meyers (1967). The comments by Massy (1966, page 3) are relevant as well. Of course there are many examples where good aggregate predictions are obtained because of the cancelling effects of individual experience. For a good discussion of these cancelling mechanisms, as well as their probable influence in marketing, see Katona (1958).

number of factors operating, as we have noted in Chapter 3. Clearly the best approach is to use all of them in concert; but notwithstanding, it is probable that attitudes will be the single best predictor, and one of the most valuable aids to diagnosing brand choice phenomena.

Because there is a significant relationship, the *shape* of the curve describing the relationship becomes interesting. In Figure 4–5 we have drawn the linear, cubic, and sixth order curves that link the attitudes and behavior of all buyers of the product. First we notice that the curve is monotonically increasing upward to the right, regardless of the degree of the polynomial. This conforms to the hypothesis developed in Chapter 2. Secondly, the curve is fairly flat, that is, whereas the mean brand choice probability is 0.52, the probability with a very favorable attitude only increases to 0.72. Clearly the environmental factors are exerting a

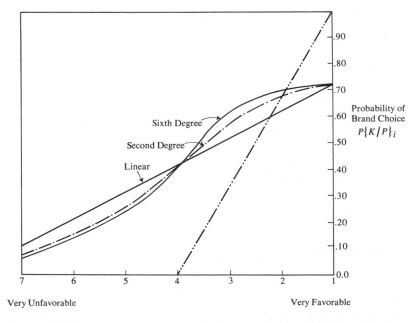

Figure 4–5. Attitude-behavior model for non-durables "Analysis" brand.

considerable impact. We will examine this issue in Chapter 5. Perhaps the feature of the curve that is most perplexing is the size of the left intercept, which implies a brand choice probability of 0.12 when the initial attitude is very unfavorable. On closer examination this turns out to be partially an artifact of the curve-fitting procedure. Briefly, what has happened is that categories 1, 2, 3, and 4 include 83 per cent of the buyers of the product, and literally swamp the households in categories 5, 6, and 7. Even the high order polynomials do not entirely account for the fact that 58 per cent of the households in the three unfavorable categories made no purchases of the analysis brand.

The analysis above was repeated for heavy and light buyer groups. Only the linear term for each of these groups has been plotted in Figure 4–6. As before, the higher orders contribute little to the definition of the relationship for these two sub-groups.

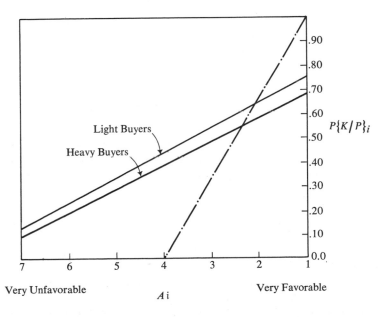

Figure 4–6. Attitude-behavior model for heavy and light buyers of a non-durables brand.

103

Keeping in mind the shaky estimate of brand choice probability for light users and the difference in attitude score distribution for heavy and light buyers (see Figure 4–4) it is encouraging that the two curves are so close. Evidently our working assumption that the slope and location of the individual brand curves, within a product class, are invariant[8] is supported by this result. The difference between the two curves, even at the right hand intercept, is less than the sum of twice the standard error of the regression coefficient for the two curves. Thus, the difference in elevation is only moderately significant. Also the simple correlation coefficients for the two groups are close: 0.489 for light buyers, and 0.512 for heavy buyers. However, we shall have to await the analysis of Chapter 5 to know if the dispersions for heavy and light buyers are the same, that is, if the proportions of these two groups in various criterion groups are similar. If the proportions are similar, we of course will conclude that purchase volume is neither an environmental factor nor a moderating effect.

Testing the Assumptions of the Attitude–Behavior Model

(A). *The Effect of Introducing Additional Dimensions and Intentions as Predictors of Behavior.* The crux of the theoretical argument in Chapter 2 was that the affective component of brand attitudes is congruent with the other attitude components, (at least in brand choice behavior). When this argument was developed it was noted that reliance on one attitude component as a predictor was contrary to widely held theories that purchase intentions have unique predictive power in buying contexts (Wells, 1961), and that "the meaning (of a concept) is richer than the evaluative content" (Osgood, 1955). With this in mind a test of the incremental predictive power of the cognitive and conative components should be of considerable interest. A further question concerns the advis-

---

8. Of course, there may be a considerable difference between brands in the distribution of probability of purchase and attitudes of the buyers of the product, but it seems that all this variability can be accommodated by the same curve relating attitude and behavior.

ability of using a unidimensional scale of affect to represent the affective or evaluative component. This is particularly an issue with the non-durables product, where an additional assumption has been made that one semantic differential scale of "general liking" will be a satisfactory approximation to an affect scale. Yet other studies of products, using a number of semantic differential scales (for example Mukherjee, 1965), have shown that the evaluative component may vary along several product oriented dimensions. For example, in the Mukherjee study four dimensions of coffee attitudes were identified—comforting quality, heartiness, genuineness, and freshness—and each dimension included cognitive and evaluative items. Given this state of affairs, the question is: How well does each respondent do in combining and weighing all these different dimensions of evaluation to come up with a single overall judgment of affect or liking–disliking?

These assumptions concerning the lack of incremental *predictive*[9] power of intentions, cognitions, and additional dimensions of the evaluative component can be tested with the non-durables analysis brand. The testing procedure started with the probability of brand choice as the dependent variable in a linear multiple regression equation, with stepwise additions of the following *independent* variables, in order of decreasing contribution to the coefficient of multiple determination (R^2):

1. "General liking" scale—seven point semantic differential scale used as single measure of affect. This scale was used to test the model of Chapter 2; see Figure 4–5.
2. Intentions to buy "analysis" brand within the next month.[10] This is a

---

9. Individual attitude items may, of course, provide considerable insight into the "reasons" for the overall liking or disliking. Recall for example, that Achenbaum (1966) relates the strategic importance of a product attribute, to the size of the correlation of that attribute's attitude item to the overall liking or disliking score.

10. This intentions measure is very similar to others in general use in marketing today. It may well be that a better measure of intentions could have been devised: for example, expanding the time horizon and including more explicit categories to get closer to the measure of probability of choice used here. This is the approach recently being taken by Juster (1966). However, it probably demands more information from the respondent than is reasonable to expect, and may actually increase guessing and non responses.

five-point scale, ranging from "definitely will, probably will, not sure one way or other, probably will not, [to] definitely will not."

3. Factor scores (in the form of standard normal deviates), for each of the following four factors, which resulted from a principal components reduction of 12 semantic differential scales, each dealing with an attribute of the product, such as "low in price—high in price."

   a. Factor 1: *General* evaluative dimension (this factor had loadings on five different attributes, but each attribute was an important feature of the product—in terms of deciding whether or not to make a purchase).

   b. Factor 2: *Specific* evaluative dimension (this factor dealt entirely with food value).

   c. Factor 3: *Activity* dimension (dynamism)—in the sense used by Osgood *et al.* (1955) as, "concerned with quickness, excitement, warmth, agitation, and the like" (page 73). This distinguishes it from intentions, which imply a different sort of future-oriented activity.

   d. Factor 4: *Cognitive* dimension, dealing primarily with perceptions as to how the product is used. As with many food products, this one could be used in a variety of ways on a number of different occasions, but users varied widely in their appraisal of the use opportunities.

The procedures by which these factor scores were developed are discussed in Appendix D. Although the four factors only accounted for 66 per cent of the variance, within the twelve scales (indicating that the attitude structure is highly complex), they provide a number of advantages which facilitate the test of the model's assumptions. First, there is the usual benefit of improved understanding of the attitude structure. It is just not possible to comprehend the meaning of twelve different scales, particularly when there are wide fluctuations in the level of association of various pairs of scales. Second, the availability of these factors permits a tie-in with the "measurement of meaning" tradition of Osgood *et al.* (1955), who pioneered the semantic differential scale. There are several interesting departures in the structure of attitudes toward this brand, as compared with the usual three factor structure found in the meaning studies: the evaluative, potency, and activity factors. The brand evaluative factor has been broken down into general and specific elements, and there is no potency factor. Of course, these parallels should not be pushed too far, since very product-specific items were used in the brand study. Lastly the reduction from twelve highly correlated items to four "statistically independent" factors minimizes collinearity. Palda (1963, page 281) indicates how important this might be in conducting the structural analysis necessary to test the assumptions of the attitude–behavior model, "Collinearity will not, per se, affect regression forecasts, although it will lead to a lowered reliability of individual parameter estimates, as it has a tendency to increase their standard error. However, if there are errors of measurement in the data, collinearity may distort seriously the coefficient estimates."

The results of the test are shown in Table 4–6, for each step of the equation as well as the final equation. The meaning of these results is clear. In fact on the most critical criteria, of

Table 4–6—Test of Incremental Value of Intention and Attitude Components as Predictors of Behavior

(A) Step-Wise Test[a]

Number of Step	Variable Added at Step	R^2 After Each Step	Standard Error of Estimate at Each Step
0	———	0.0	0.3881
1	"General liking" scale	0.242	0.3381
2	Intentions	0.251	0.337
3	Factor 2: Specific evaluative dimension	0.258	0.3361
4	Factor 4: Cognitive dimension	0.263	0.336
5	Factor 1: General evaluative dimension	0.263	0.337
6	Factor 3: Activity dimension	0.263	0.337

(B) Final Multiple Regression Equation
(Probability of brand choice is dependent variable)

Variable	Partial Correlation Coefficient	Beta Weight	Significance Level — T Test (218 degrees of freedom)
"General liking" scale	−0.331	−0.471	$P < 0.001$
Intentions	−0.095	−0.105	$P < 0.15$
Factor 2	−0.1160	−0.101	$P < 0.08$
Factor 4	0.074	0.082	$P < 0.30$
Factor 1	−0.015	−0.014	not significant
Factor 3	−0.003	−0.003	not significant

a A better overall measure of the effectiveness of these variables might be Theil's U (coefficient of inequality). This inequality provides a test of predictive performance, with $U = 0$ for perfect forecasts, whereas values close to 1.0 indicate bad forecasting. (See Palda, 1963, page 287). While more experience with this measure is necessary a good marketing forecast might have a U value of 0.10 to 0.15 with poor ones, that is not usable, from 0.50 upwards to 1.0. The multiple regression equation in Table 4–6 was used to calculate a Theil's U of 0.276, indicating reasonably satisfactory performance.

ability of reduce dispersion (that is, contribute information), none of the added variables is of any use whatsoever. This is very strong support for the hypothesis that affect is congruent with intentions, as well as the other cognitive and "dynamic" components of attitudes.

(*B*) *Testing other measures of buying behavior.* Thus far, in our empirical and theoretical examinations of behavior, we have concentrated on *choice decisions* as a probabilistic process. However there are many other kinds of behavior, some of which were discussed in Chapter 2. The non-durables panel data provides a means of testing two alternative measures of behavior. One is specific to the product class and cannot be described because of the need to maintain the disguise. The other, which is the *proportion of total units bought*, that were accounted for by the "analysis" brand, is of general interest. For example, it might be argued that a purchase of a "giant" package of detergent is several times more important than the purchase of a small trial package of the same kind of detergent,[11] even though each is a separate brand choice decision. Such a behavior measure is easily adapted to this problem by (1) assigning standard units to each purchase according to the amount purchased, (2) summing these units across all purchases made by the household during the panel, and (3) dividing the number of units of the "analysis" brand that were purchased, by the total units, to get the proportion.

This was done for the non-durables product without notable results. The correlation of the two behavior measures (choice decisions versus units purchased) was 0.78. When the latter measure was used as the dependent variable, in the multiple regression equation of Table 4–6, the coefficient of multiple determination declined from 0.263 to 0.157 and the standard error of estimate jumped from 0.337 to 0.461. A good bit of this poor showing can be traced to the extreme dispersion (and consequent instability) of the proportion of units purchased. In

---

11. It was this problem, among others, that led Rohloff (1963) to develop the gain-loss approach to measuring brand switching.

general it seems that purchase volume is confounded by even more variables than the decision process, and is not a valid measure to try and predict with an initial attitude.

Summary

In this chapter we tested a number of hypotheses derived from the development of a model of the attitude–behavior relationship for brand choice situations. Two sets of panel data, describing very different product categories, were used for this purpose. Within the limitations of both sets of data, and the considerable problems of inter-product comparison, the validity of the model has been demonstrated—although certainly not firmly established. Specifically, the tests of this chapter indicate:

That the attitude–behavior relationship is monotonically increasing, as the attitude improves;

That the affective component is a sufficient measure of brand attitudes (including intentions), at least for the purpose of predicting brand choice behavior in a product category with a short repurchase cycle;

That the slope of the relationship of attitudes and behavior *probably* increases as the purchase cycle shortens, indicating that the environmental factors have lessened influence. This was only tested at the aggregate level, hence the inference should be made cautiously;

That moderating effects are very influential, in view of the large proportion of variance left unexplained. The next chapter will be directed toward understanding the nature and probable influence of some of these influences, and;

That the probability based measure of brand choice decisions is the most satisfactory measure of behavior.

In conclusion, the model provides a useful structure for describing the attitude–behavior relationship; but the true test will come when it is applied to other product categories. Results may well be better for larger samples, and certainly could be improved by the use of attitude scales that do not bunch favorable respondents into the extreme category (see for example the efforts of

Abrams, 1966). The over-riding problem in any further tests will always be the reduction of the respondent's sensitivity to the brand by virtue of the initial attitude question. Fortunately a number of precautions are possible (see, for instance, Roper, 1961, page 522), and memory decay over the duration of the panel works very much toward ensuring reliable purchase results. As Appendix C shows, the purchase results are reliable when compared to a parallel panel which was not asked to provide brand attitudes at the beginning. On these grounds a marketing decision-maker can have confidence in the implications of this model for the source and strength of loyalty toward his brand. More generally, he can use brand attitudes with some feeling that the predictions are better than those obtained from other, more remote variables, and certainly are capable of as many insights. These advantages are increasingly diluted as the purchase cycle lengthens, because predictions of brand choice behavior become obscured by the effects of environmental factors. Nonetheless, for most consumer non-durables, the attitude–behavior relationship is of such relevance and productive of so many insights, that all prospects of the "neobehaviorist revival" feared by Bauer (1966, page 6) should be vigorously resisted.

Chapter 5

Further Empirical Results:
Influences on the Attitude—
Behavior Relationship

Having described the relationship between brand attitudes and brand choice behavior, the next step is to improve our understanding of the nature of the relationship. The approach is first to look for the presence of environmental factors which dampen the behavioral manifestation of attitudes. These factors include exposure to new information, the competitive effect of similar brands and interferences from price, lack of availability, time pressure, overall financial constraints, and the influence of family decision processes. To the extent that these environmental factors do not account for the observed relationship, we will look for the causes of inconsistency or error in the presence of *moderating effects*. These effects include buying style, attitude stability, and extraneous determinants of response.

The analysis strategy, by which the presence and effect of the environmental factors and moderating effects can be identified, was developed in Chapter 3. Ideally we would like to first compare Groups I and II (as shown in Figure 5–1, which is a reproduction of Figure 3–1 placed here for convenience), to limit the focus to the environmental factors as much as possible—and then look at the residual to the attitude–behavior relationship (u_i) to identify specific moderating effects. This "ideal" strategy will be followed in the analysis of the non-durables data. Unfortunately it cannot be applied directly to the durables data, because the aggregation within attitude categories makes it impossible to distinguish consistent from inconsistent behavior. Consequently only two criterion groups of appliance buyers can be identified: those who bought a brand that they liked, and those who bought a brand which they initially disliked or were neutral toward. These groups will be influenced by environmental factors and moderating effects simultaneously.

This brief outline of the analysis strategy to be followed in this chapter conceals a number of practical problems, each with considerable potential for obscuring the influences we are seeking. Before discussing the actual findings and their implications we will briefly survey these problems with a view to appraising the potential of the techniques used here to contribute to our understanding of the numerous influences on the attitude–behavior relationship.

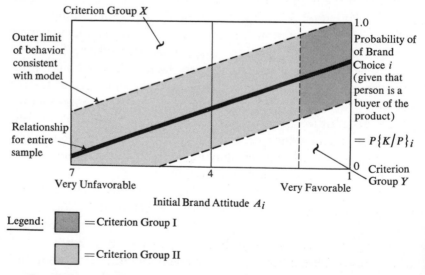

Figure 5–1. Influence of moderating effects and environmental factors.

112

Problems Inherent in the Analysis Strategy

The problems to be encountered in the remainder of this chapter are common to most attempts to understand rich bodies of data from cross-section surveys. The only redeeming feature of this study is that we are not attempting to project our results as representative of any other population than the one from which the data are drawn, and hence are spared some of the problems of estimation when measurement errors and sampling variations must be taken into account. Otherwise the problems follow those noted by Morgan and Sonquist[1] in a very useful account of the nature of survey data:

1. Many of the explanatory variables to be used are *classifications*, with different measurement properties, that is, some are interval measures, others are ordinal, and so forth. "Even when the measures seem to be continuous . . . such as age or income, there is good reason to believe that their effects are not linear. For instance, people earn their highest incomes in the middle age ranges."

2. There is known to be a high degree of *intercorrelation* between certain classes of explanatory variables, particularly between demographic variables such as education, occupation, and income. "This makes it difficult to assess the relative importance of different [explanatory] factors, since their intercorrelations get in the way." This is perhaps the most serious problem, given our interest in appraising structural influences, rather than predicting some kind of performance.

3. Many sets of variables *interact* with each other, rather than combine additively. This happens not only because this is the way the world is put together, but also because several explanatory variables may appear in the same theoretical construct, or serve as proxies for more than one construct. The arbitrary creation of a family life cycle is perhaps the most common example of an attempt to account for interactions; in this case between age, marital status, presence, and age of children.

4. Morgan and Sonquist mention several other problems which are of lesser importance in this study, but can never be forgotten when it is time to appraise the results. These problems concern errors in measures (and the lack of evidence as to the size of the errors, or the extent to which they are random), errors due to sampling variability, and the place of the variable

---

1. All quotations are from Morgan and Sonquist (1963, pages 415–420).

in a chain of causation. On this last point, "some of the predicting characteristics are logically prior to others in the sense that they can cause them
but cannot be affected by them."

Finally, all these problems deal with the problems of analyzing
the data as it exists. But all the analysis is to no avail if the measures
do not represent the theoretical constructs. This requires that the
theoretical construct itself be stated in very explicit terms, and that
its operational counterpart represent that construct and no other.
There are a number of instances in the rest of this chapter where
these goals are comprised. Some of the theoretical constructs are
speculative, in other cases there was no variable that directly tapped
the construct, and sometimes it was necessary to compromise on
the quality of the explanatory variable because there was no work-
able alternative. This may well be the greatest weakness in the
analysis of this chapter, because it necessitates an unreasonable
amount of inference about the nature of some influences and
reduces the opportunities to make comparisons between the
durables and the non-durables results.

Possible Analysis Techniques and Their Limitations

This is not designed to be a review of all the analysis options
that are open for the structural analysis of two or more groups
with a large number of intercorrelated, interacting explanatory
variables. Briefly, a step-by-step application of techniques will be
described which resolves, in a reasonably satisfactory way, most of
the problems discussed above *except* for interaction effects. The
spirit, if not the result, of the endeavor has been well expressed by
Binder:

> We must use all available weapons of attack, face our problems realistically
> and not retreat to the land of fashionable sterility, learn to sweat over our
> data with an admixture of judgment and intuitive rumination, and accept the
> usefulness of particular data even when the level of analysis available for them
> is markedly below that available for other data in the empirical area.[2]

Much can be learned by taking the explanatory variables one at a

---

2. Binder (1964, page 294).

time, keeping in mind the extent to which they are intercorrelated. However, even with two groups to compare the mind is soon overloaded, and the net result is primarily impressionistic. This is particularly true when it comes to deciding which of the explanatory variables exerts the most influence.

What we wish to do next is either reduce the number of variables, without losing explanatory power, or consider all the variables simultaneously with due respect for the intercorrelations. This immediately suggests multivariate statistical techniques, such as factor analysis and multiple discriminant analysis. Their use is contingent on a satisfactory solution of the first problem: that of many of the variables being classifications rather than continuous variables.[3] The usual approach is to build up arbitrary scales, which have quasi-interval properties. This is often done with occupation, by ranking all occupations and then assigning the numbers one, two, three, and so on to each occupation group. Perhaps a better, although equally arbitrary, approach is to create indices that summarize several variables (see Lazarsfeld and Barton, 1951), on a unidimensional scale. The best we can expect are quasi-interval measures; but these are usually adequate when the emphasis is on the degree of covariation between two variables.

The main analytical tool used in this chapter is multiple discriminant analysis, because it takes intercorrelations among explanatory variables into consideration. Unfortunately this technique introduces several new problems in the course of resolving the question of intercorrelations. Before these problems are reviewed we will discuss the statistical rationale briefly and indicate how the results are to be interpreted.

Multiple discriminant analysis. This technique is sometimes described as multiple regression analysis with a multichotomous dependent variable. Both regression and discriminant analysis use, "a linear combination of numerical values for two or more independent variables . . . to predict the behavior of a dependent variable." (Massy, 1962, page 95).

---

3. Morgan and Sonquist suggest the use of dummy variables to overcome this problem. So far it has only been applied to regression analysis (Suits, 1957).

Two-way discriminant analysis, which deals with two mutually exclusive groups, is most commonly used in marketing problems. The data that are used consist of the means of all the variables in both groups, and the elements of the common dispersion matrix. The technique (see Hoel, 1954, page 180) determines the linear function of all the independent variables that minimizes the overlap in the distributions for the two groups.[4] Specifically, a function

$$Y = ax_1 + bx_2 + \cdots, + kx_k$$

is calculated which minimizes the within group sum of squares and maximizes the between group sum of squares (where Y is a dummy variable reflecting group membership, $X_1 \ldots X_k$ are the independent variables and a, b, $\ldots$, k are the discriminant coefficients). The solution requires that the independent variables are approximately normally distributed in each group, the respective dispersion matrices are roughly equal, and the group memberships are known in advance. These requirements can be troublesome on occasion, but the decision on how to treat them is largely judgmental. On the other hand, there is no escaping the linearity and additivity assumptions imposed on the data in order to make the analysis manageable. If there are strong *a priori* grounds for believing that key relationships in a body of data are non-linear, and multiplicative (or interact strongly), then this technique may not be appropriate.

Interpretation of discriminant coefficients. Each coefficient represents the contribution of the associated explanatory variable towards distinguishing one group from another, or alternatively, the effect on the probability that an individual belongs to one criterion group rather than another. Before the *relative* contribution of each variable can be evaluated it is necessary to standardize each coefficient by multiplying it by the standard deviation of the associated variable. These standardized coefficients are analogous to Beta coefficients in multiple regression analysis, in that they are expressed in terms of equally likely changes (King, 1967).

---

4. This procedure has been generalized for N groups. A brief description is given in Massy (1965, pages 41–47).

These discriminant coefficients are more sensitive measures of group differences than a table comparing the group means of the variables for several reasons. First, "the coefficients take into account correlations among variables. For example, since older people obviously have fewer children living at home, the means for these two variables would tend to be highly correlated from group to group. The discriminant coefficient, on the other hand, gives us the effect of number of children at home, holding age constant, and vice versa" (Massy, 1965, page 43).

Second, it is often the case that a variable will have the same mean value in both groups, and appear to be insignificant when analyzed by the usual univariate procedures, but have a large and influential discriminant coefficient. The reason for this may be readily seen from Figure 5–2 (see Cooley and Lohnes, 1962, page 121) which considers the entire profile. This figure shows two negatively correlated variables A and B, where there is no difference between the means of Groups I and II on variable B. The discriminant function (0–0) for these two variables would use the relation between A and B to minimize the overlap between the two groups, resulting in a high loading for variable B.

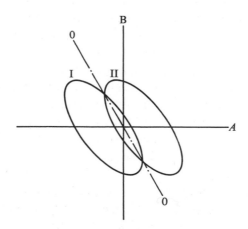

Figure 5–2. *Contribution of dispersion to description of differences between means.*

Third, the discriminant coefficients can be used to provide a simple index of the aggregate similarity of many groups by means of a "confusion" matrix. This matrix describes the pattern of misclassifications by comparing the *known* group membership of each individual with the *assigned* group value according to the individual's discriminant scores.[5] If an individual is known, *a priori*, to belong in Group I, but is assigned to Group II because of his discriminant score, then he has been misclassified. Confusion matrices become increasingly useful as the number of groups increase. The proportion of misclassifications of the members of a group provides an indication of the relative distinctiveness of that group. If there are many misclassifications it is instructive to see which group they were assigned to, for these groups are probably quite similar along the measured variables.

Interpretation of the coefficients may be confounded if variables that contribute to the definition of the groups are left out of the discriminant function, or there is significant multicollinearity (the independent variables are highly correlated among themselves). When important variables are neglected the estimates of all coefficients will be biased to the extent that the associated variables are correlated with the neglected variable. The most satisfactory way to avoid this problem is to develop a careful and comprehensive theoretical understanding of the problem, and refer to relevant empirical work, to ensure that no variables are neglected. Multicollinearity, "reduces the efficiency of the estimates (of the coefficients) because . . . the amount of information about the effect of each independent variable, taken separately, declines as the intercorrelations increase" (Massy, 1962, page 93). At the extreme the separate influences of two variables, on the definition of the groups, are completely overshadowed as the correlation between the two approaches one. The usual solution is to compute a reduced set of uncorrelated variables (factors) from the original set of correlated explanatory variables. A principal components

---

5. A discriminant score (Z) for a given respondent is computed by summing the product of the discriminant coefficient for each variable times the value of the variable for the household, across all the variables in the equation.

solution[6] with varimax rotation is the method generally chosen for this purpose, and will be used as such in this report. Even when multicollinearity is not an issue it is often useful for subsequent analysis to have an unwieldy list of variables reduced to more manageable proportions.

Statistical tests. Before one can have confidence in statements about the relative importance of specific coefficients it is necessary to demonstrate that the observed results did not arise by chance. Several procedures have been developed to test the null hypothesis that the means of all explanatory variables are the same in the two groups. Conceptually this requires a measure of the generalized distance between any two groups (i.e. Mahalanobis D^2), and a test of the significance of this distance that considers the degrees of freedom available in the two groups.[7] These tests can usually be generalized to the case of N groups.

It is tempting to use the efficiency of the classification procedure as a test of the effectiveness of the discriminant function. Various procedures, such as those discussed by Bush and Mosteller (1954), are available to test the significance of the difference between the proportion of respondents that were correctly classified and the proportion correct that would be expected by chance. However, Frank, Massy, and Morrison (1965, page 252) warn that such tests will be biased if they are applied to the same sample of data as

---

6. Lawley and Maxwell (1963, page 2) show that the principal components solution is the most appropriate means of reducing data structures in the absence of any hypotheses about the nature of the structure. The occasions when the use of this, or any other factor analytic technique, may be invalid have been discussed by Carroll (1961) and Guilford (1952).

A study by the author (Day, 1968) indicates that the benefits of principal components analysis (as a precursor to multiple discriminant analysis) may be outweighed by the loss of predictive information during the process of reducing the data. The alternative of non-metric scaling appears to more satisfactory on a number of criteria.

7. "Mahalanbois D^2 is proportional to the generalized T^2 statistic. The proportionality constant is a function of the degrees of freedom available in the two samples. Both statistics can be easily transformed so that they are distributed as F under the null hypothesis of no difference between the mean vectors (Morrison *et al.*, 1966, page 86).

was used to estimate the discriminant coefficients. The kind of bias that results because the discriminant function is the best "fit" to the sample data, and hence maximizes the predictive power of the function for that body of data, cannot be avoided. The bias that results from the analyst's "search" for the best subset of explanatory variables, from a larger original set, can be avoided simply by not searching or by reducing the original list of variables by factor analysis or index construction. If split sample validation is used the amount of bias present is equal to the shrinkage in predictive efficacy (proportion of misclassifications) that is found when coefficients estimated with one set of data are applied to a new set.[8]

The treatment of interactions. Several methods of allowing for interactions between variables (other than index construction) were considered—and rejected with considerable regret. Because of the large number of variables it was not feasible to use variance analysis to look directly for interaction effects, or to evaluate the effect of "intensifier" attributes as suggested by Coleman (1964, page 226), because of disappearing cell sizes and the extreme loss of information that would result if many of the variables were dichotomized or trichotomized. Without knowing in advance which explanatory variables might interact to a significant degree in the analysis it is obviously impossible to build variables that exhaust all possible interactions, or to run separate analyses on the two parts of a dichotomy separately when it is known that the dichotomy is involved in most of the interactions. The most attractive method is the *Automatic Interaction Detector* Program developed by Sonquist and Morgan.[9] The rejection of this alternative, which provides results similar to discriminant analysis, was unavoidable because the algorithm is such that the minimum sample size feasible is approximately one thousand. For a large

8. The shrinkage can be considerable. In one study (Frank, Massy, and Morrison, 1964, page 322) the proportion of correct classifications was 67.9 per cent in the analysis sample and 54.6 per cent in the validation sample.

9. "The basic idea is the sequential identification and segregation of subgroups one at a time, nonsymmetrically, so as to select the set of subgroups which will reduce the error in predicting the dependent variable as much as possible relative to the number of groups" (Sonquist and Morgan, 1964, page 430).

number of variables the optimal sample size would seem to be more than two thousand. This procedure is strongly recommended as an effective solution to many of the problems of analysis outlined at the beginning of this chapter if the sample size requirements can be met.

Analysis of the Durables Data

From the analysis of Chapter 4, two durables criterion groups were defined as:

I. Appliance buyers who bought a brand that they originally favored. This group comprised the 30 buyers who had an attitude score between 0 and 1.9 (this included all favorable and extremely favorable attitudes) towards one of the seven major brands included in the brand attitudes question.

II. Appliance buyers who bought a brand which they initially disliked or were neutral toward. This group includes the remaining 19 of the 49 buyers for which brand attitude and behavior information were available.

Recall that another 70 panel members made at least one appliance purchase but could not be used as part of the analysis because they did not purchase one of the seven major brands included in the brand attitude question. Consequently the small size of Criterion Group I, compared to Group II, is probably not at all representative of the true situation—even within the panel. The reason is simple; many of the purchases not included in this analysis were of lesser-known brands that the buyer might not have heard of or seen before the purchase decision period. This may be a severe limitation on the test for the presence of environmental factors, as it is just these brands that benefit most from the influence of the environment.

Description of Explanatory Variables[10]

One of the problems raised in the previous discussion of analysis strategy was the difficulty of obtaining empirical measures

---

10. These variables are classified in greater detail in Appendix E.

that adequately represent the theoretical constructs thought to be relevant. The purpose of this section is to describe the rationale behind each explanatory variable in terms of the environmental factor or moderating effect it is supposed to represent.

Six of the 14 variables to be described are factors resulting from the reduction of a set of nine "demographic" variables and a second set of eight "information" variables. The input variables to the two factor analyses are described in Appendix E (Tables E–1, E–2, and E–3). In the following discussion these six factors will be described according to their component variables, and the number of the factor in the order it was extracted.[11] The order of presentation of the variables will follow the organization of Chapter 3, where the theoretical constructs were developed.

(A) ENVIRONMENTAL FACTORS

I. *Exposure to new information.* A large number of possible measures were considered in Chapter 3 that could be used to infer that respondents in Criterion Group II were more generally exposed to brand oriented information that caused them to reappraise their initial attitude. The empirical analogues to these measures that are available for the analysis of appliance buyers are.

Exposure to print (magazines and newspapers) media; this is INFO FACTOR Number One.

Degree of preference for print media versus television; this is INFO FACTOR Number Two.

Desire for shopping oriented information (and assistance); this is INFO FACTOR Number Three.

---

11. For example: DEMO-FACTOR Number Two is the second factor extracted from the list of nine demographic variables. Because latent roots are extracted in descending order of magnitude, the factors (or latent vectors) are presented in order of the amount of total variance absorbed. Even though a factor accounts for a great deal of variance we cannot infer that it is any more important than the other factors in explaining a particular problem.

It should be noted that DEMO-FACTOR Number One is not included in the discriminant analysis. This factor turned out to be general socio-economic status which has no counterpart in the theoretical constructs. (See Appendix E for an exact description of this factor.)

Number of changes[12] reported by the household during the six months duration of the panel. This measure is based on the notion that important changes in family circumstances lead to new needs and a reappraisal of old attitudes in a somewhat different information environment.

Number of additions to appliance inventory, and number of products needing repair or adjustment. It is assumed here that direct product experience leads to the acquisition of new information; the greater the number of acquisitions the more shopping that was done, the higher the frequency of repairs and adjustments the better the chance that the respondent discussed appliance brands with friends and repairmen, and so forth.

There was no variable to measure the possibility that time pressures felt by the respondent reduced the number of opportunities to obtain new information. One vaguely related measure is the stage in the married life cycle; on the supposition that older couples with no children have more free time and flexibility than young couples with young children. This measure has much broader implications than this, of course.

II. *Opportunities to make brand choices.* As we noted in Chapter 3, this environmental factor is difficult to infer from indirect evidence. One plausible approach considers differences between urban and rural residents in the likelihood of exposure to unknown or poorly rated brands. The distribution of appliance brands is such that the rural buyer is usually faced with a local selection from very few brands (although he may buy from a catalogue or travel some distance to broaden his choice). The urban buyer, on the other hand, has easy access to all kinds of brands—at regular and discount prices—and therefore is more liable to be classified in Criterion Group II. Of course, by only asking about reasonably well known brands we limit the opportunity to test this hypothesis fully.

There is some support for the distinction between urban and rural dwellers in degree of access to brands, in a question on the process of decision-making. This question, which is not particularly valid because of a high non-response rate, shows that re-

---

12. The following possible changes were included in the total: people entering or leaving household; change in employment of head and/or respondent; change in residence; change in mortgage payments; change in income or change in savings.

spondents in Criterion Group II were more likely to have decided on the stores to be visited before deciding on the brand, product, and price range. From the argument above we would explain the need to decide on the store first by the fact that this group has more stores and more brands to choose among (see Table 5–1).

There is some indirect evidence which can be used to link the size of the largest brand cluster[13] to past opportunities to make brand choices. Because it is widely believed that appliance brand loyalty is low (see Newman, 1966) the presence of a large brand cluster may simply be an indication that the household had few opportunities to buy other brands. This argument is admittedly tenuous, both for the past as well as for the future. However the variable has considerable practical utility, despite its shortcomings in this particular context.

III. *Price and financial constraints.* A preliminary test of price as a environmental factor was reported in Chapter 4 (see Table 4–2). Attitudes were shown to be very poor predictors of appliance brand choice in product categories costing more than $75.00, but very satisfactory at lower price levels. Unfortunately it is not

Table 5–1—Process of Decision-Making by Appliance Buyers
(Percentages are based on individual purchases)

	Criterion Group I	Criterion Group II
Decide on first		
Store	28%	39%
Price range	22	11
Brand or product	50	50
	100%	100%
Decide on next		
Store	44%	28%
Price range	46	60
Brand or product	10	12
	100%	100%
Base= number of purchases:	42	18
Purchases for which no data on decision process was collected	25	23

13. Number of products in the largest brand cluster in the inventory, as a percentage of the total number of products for which the brand is known.

feasible to use price paid as an environmental factor, because of the many product categories, and the difficulty of deciding whether the price was high or low for the particular category. In Chapter 3 it was suggested that economic constraints (such as lack of income and/or available cash) would be an appropriate environmental factor in the case of appliances; in those situations where the constraint is severe it is probable that the brand name has very little influence. This variable is tapped by DEMO FACTOR Number Three, which is a weighted combination of expected change in family income, as a percentage of total income, and the amount of savings, investments, or reserve funds (see Appendix E: Table E–3).

IV. *Family decision processes.* A question was available to test this hypothesis directly. Since it was a dichotomous question it was not incorporated as an independent variable in the discriminant analysis. The results from this variable, reported in Table 5–2, are mildly (but not significantly) contradictory to the hypothesis. That is, we would have expected a lower proportion of the panel respondents in Criterion Group II to have participated in the selection of the brand.

V. *Attraction of competing brands.* There is no variable available that will test this hypothesis in this context. First it is impossible to define the competing brands. Second, we have assumed that the influence of competing brands is entirely inhibiting and thus will not show a differential effect between Criterion Groups I and II.

(B) MODERATING EFFECTS

I. *Buying style.* There were no explanatory variables available

Table 5–2—Family Decision Processes-Appliance Buyers
(Percentage of total in group in brackets)

	Criterion Group I	Criterion Group II
Respondent helped select the brand	22 (74%)	15 (79%)
Respondent did not help to select the brand	8 (26%)	4 (21%)
Total	30	19

to define the appropriate modes of behavior. This is only likely to be a serious shortcoming with dimensions such as economy-consciousness or time pressure, as neither impulsiveness nor the level of ambiguity have much relevance to appliance buying where the purchase cycle is so long. It would have been useful to have some measure of innovativeness, because an individual's willingness to entertain new product concepts or internalize product information is likely to be tempered by this characteristic. In fact the entire innovation research tradition is most relevant to high risk acquisitions like appliances.

II. *Attitude stability*. Two approaches are possible: One assumes that a buyer's attitudes become firmer as experience with the product cumulates, the other avoids any inferences by having the respondent rate her own confidence in the attitude judgment. Only the first measure is available in this situation, in the form of the size of the household's appliance inventory. It should be recognized that this measure is open to contamination from product experience that newlyweds may have had before their household was formed (and not reflected in the inventory), and is inflated by gifts from the outside. Also this measure gives equal weights to small hand appliances such as irons, and to major appliances such as freezers. On balance these distortions should cancel themselves within criterion groups. A more questionable measure of experience is the number of appliance brands the respondent can recall without assistance (unaided recall). Despite the shortcomings of this variable, primarily due to the reliance on memory, it seemed advisable to include it because of its wide application in marketing research.

III. *Extraneous determinants of response*. There is some risk attached to incorporating measures of extraneous determinants in the analysis. Of necessity we have to rely on inferences about irregularities or consistent biases in the pattern of attitude responses. Inevitably such measures will be associated with the brand attitude score which was used to partition the sample into criterion groups. This raises the possibility that the discriminant coefficient for the measure of extraneous determinants will be spurious, that

126

is, an artifact of the design of the analysis. To emphasize the speculative aspect of these measures it seems a reasonable precaution to make separate analyses, with and without these measures. By comparing the Mahalanobis D^2 statistic for both analyses we will have an index of the incremental discriminating power of these measures without distorting the discriminant coefficients of the other explanatory variables in the function. The measures of the extraneous determinants of appliance brand attitudes are the average attitude toward the brands that were not purchased (usually six brands), and the range of attitudes between the highest rated and the worst rated of the seven brands. This variable is conceivably distorted, because the "range" overlooks a great deal of information contained in the frequency distribution, and even if correct, it may be more of a reflection of the respondent's ability to discriminate among appliance brands than of the structure of the attitude.

IV. *Other moderating effects.* Test theorists have found that age and education are often useful. They have not been included in this analysis because there is no *a priori* reason for their inclusion, and the aggregative test on the durables data makes it difficult to separate the moderating effects from the environmental factors.

The Results of the Durables Analysis

The first run was made without including the measures of extraneous determinants[14] (see Table 5–3). Overall the results are not exciting; the two groups are different, but the differences are not sharp. There is a considerable disparity between the weak F test and the robust classification performance. We noted before that the percentage of "hits" is liable to be biased upwards because the same data are used to estimate the discriminant coefficients and the efficiency of classification. However other users of discriminant analysis have found that the F test is a very conservative

---

14. The univariate differences between groups for all the variables used in the analysis can be found in Appendix E, Table E-4.

test of the distance between groups when the sample size is very small, as it is in this situation.

Thus while the results can be said to be provocative and meaningful, they should not be accepted with unbounded enthusiasm. So far as specific results are concerned, we can say the Criterion Group II (buyers of brands that were not initially favored) differs from Criterion Group I as follows:

1. Contrary to the hypothesis about exposure to new information, Criterion Group II is much *less* interested in obtaining shopping oriented information (and assistance). At the same time this group is exposed to less print media.

Table 5–3—Run I: Comparison of Two Criterion Groups of Appliance Buyers

(Excluding measures of extraneous determinants)

Description of Variable	Standardized Discriminant Coefficients (Ranked in descending order)
1. Desire for shopping oriented information	−1.000
2. Anticipated economic constraints	−0.730
3. Exposure to print media	−0.701
4. Access to stores	+0.596
5. Number of changes during the time of the panel	+0.558
6. Married life cycle	−0.530
7. Number of products in appliance inventory	+0.495
8. Number of inventory additions	−0.462
9. Size of largest brand cluster	−0.450
10. Choice of print media versus TV	−0.280
11. Repair experience	−0.007

STATISTICAL TESTS

$F(11, 37) = 1.259$ Significant: $P < 0.25$
Mahalanobis $D^2 = 1.513$
Efficiency of classification ("confusion" matrix)

	Predicted Group Membership		
	I	II	Total
Actual criterion group *membership* I	13	6	19
II	6	24	30
Total	19	30	49

Percentage "hits": 1. discriminant function = 75.5%
2. chance[15] = 52.5

Degree of improvement   23.0%

15. See Bush and Mosteller (1954) for a procedure that estimates chance assignment in multi-fold tables. Statistical tests are available, but are not appropriate here.

This cannot, of course, disprove the basic hypothesis, as we do not know what actually happened at the time of purchase. However, it certainly raises serious doubts and suggests that the effects of information are more complex than was anticipated.

2. As expected, Criterion Group II is much more constrained by the family finances, and therefore is likely to be more price conscious. Oddly enough, this is not supported by the data on the process of decision-making (Table 5–1), which show that this group was less likely to decide on the price range before deciding on the store and brand.

3. The data in Table 5–1 are more consistent with the hypothesis that Criterion Group II has better access to stores, and to a variety of brands and prices.

4. Other, less significant results that supported the initial hypotheses are the findings that Criterion Group II made more changes during the time of the panel, and are more likely to be young families with children.

5. Some contrary, but also not very significant results were that respondents in Criterion Group II have more products in their inventory (and consequently the largest brand cluster is smaller) and made fewer additions to the appliance inventory.

This picture changes somewhat when the variables dealing with the extraneous determinants (notably the possibility of an acquiescence set) are added to the discriminant function. Not only are the group differences more pronounced, but the rankings of the explanatory variables change and a few less important variables actually work in the opposite direction. The change in the rankings of the explanatory variables is due to differing degrees of relationship (or co-variation) with the added variables. Each discriminant coefficient measures the effect of the associated variable with all other variables held constant (see Table 5–4).

Whether or not these new results are taken at face value, there is an impressive effect due to differences in "response" styles. Respondents in Criterion Group II have significantly less favorable attitudes toward all other appliance brands, and see fewer differences between brands[16] (expressed as the difference in attitude

16. The following differences in group means are interesting:

	Group I	Group II
Average attitude	1.94	2.44
Range of attitudes towards brands	3.79	2.87

score between the best and least liked brands in the set of seven). This effect is so pronounced as to make the differences between groups highly significant, and have the extraneous determinants overshadow all other explanatory variables. However when extraneous determinants exert such an effect they can hardly be called "extraneous" any longer. This may indeed be the most important finding of this analysis, and certainly is on a par with the support that most of the original hypotheses received.

Perhaps the answer can be found by looking back to the results

Table 5-4—Run 2: Comparison of Two Criterion Groups of Appliance Buyers

(Including measures of extraneous determinants)

Description of Variable	Standardized Discriminant Coefficients (Ranked in descending order)
1. Average attitude toward brands that were not purchased	+1.000
2. Range of brand attitudes	−0.721
3. Anticipated economic constraints	−0.504
4. Number of changes during the time of the panel	+0.480
5. Desire for shopping oriented information	−0.358
6. Number of inventory additions	−0.346
7. Access to stores	+0.290
8. Number of products in appliance inventory	−0.288
9. Choice of print media versus TV	−0.138
10. Married life cycle	+0.132
11. to 14. The remaining variables had coefficients less than 0.050 and are of no significance.	

STATISTICAL TESTS

$F (14, 34) = 2.354$ Significant: $P > 0.03$

Efficiency of classification ("confusion" matrix)

		Predicted group membership		
		I	II	Total
Actual criterion group membership	I	12	7	19
	II	0	30	30
	Total	12	37	49

Percentage "hits": 1. discriminant function = 86.0%
2. chance   52.5

Degree of improvement   33.5%

of Chapter 4. The tentative conclusion at that juncture was that the relatively mild relationship between appliance brand attitudes and brand choice behavior was due to the dominating influence of the environmental factors. This further analysis does not refute this conclusion, but suggests that the environmental factors are influencing brand attitudes that have little cognitive content and hence are extremely susceptible to extraneous determinants. Before generalizing this conclusion to all brand attitudes it is important to note that appliance brand attitudes represent an extreme situation, because the purchase cycle is very long. The conclusion may turn out to be less valid when the buyer has numerous opportunities to reappraise her brand preference structure. For some insights into this problem, as well as further tests of the basic hypotheses about environmental factors and moderating effects, we turn to the non-durables panel results.

Analysis of the Non-Durables Data

This analysis is not constrained by an inability to estimate brand choice probabilities. As a consequence we are able to define the two criterion groups that are consistent with the model (see Figure 5–1), as well as calculate the residual (u_i) of the attitude–behavior relationship. Our testing procedure will proceed to use this information in the following tests:

I. The two largest moderating effects will be used to segment the buyers of the product into six homogeneous subgroups. The attitude–behavior relationship will then be reestimated for each of the six sub-groups. In this way the role of environmental influences on buyers with different latent structures can be evaluated.

II. To maintain comparability with the durables analysis the information about consistency with the model will be disregarded in this test, and buyers of the brand will be separated into two groups, according to whether their initial attitude was more or less favorable than λ. These two groups will be compared on

131

the relevant explanatory variables, as with the durables analysis.

III. Finally, the two consistent criterion groups will be directly compared in order to highlight the role of the environmental factors. However, it should be noted that the process of defining these two criterion groups (of buyers of the brand) also defines three other groups—one of which is made up of non-buyers of the brand. This presents an interesting additional area of analysis, in which all five groups can be simultaneously compared. Before the possibilities of this kind of an analysis can be appreciated it is necessary to define the criterion groups in more detail, and review the explanatory variables that were used.

Definition of Criterion Groups

The assignment of respondents to criterion groups closely followed the partitioning shown in Figure 5–1. The sample of 220 buyers of the product was divided as follows:

Criterion Group I ($n_1 = 84$): Buyers of the product, with a favorable or extremely favorable attitude toward the analysis brand, who *chose* the analysis brand more than 50 per cent of the time.

Criterion Group II ($n_2 = 43$): Buyers who initially disliked or were neutral toward the analysis brand, but chose it at least 30 per cent of the time.[17]

Criterion Group X ($n_x = 19$): This group deviated from the model by not initially liking the analysis brand, and then purchasing it more than 50 per cent of the time.

Criterion Group Y ($n_y = 24$): This group also deviated from the model, but in a direction opposite to Group X. Although the respondents in this group were initially favorable, or even extremely favorable, toward the analysis brand, they chose the brand less than 50 per cent of the time. In fact, ten of the 24 respondents in this group didn't buy the analysis brand at all.

Non-buyers ($n = 50$): Respondents in this group were also consistent with the model, since they did not like the analysis brand and did not buy it at all. This group will be used very little in the subsequent analysis.

---

17. A range of values was necessary to take into account differences in initial attitude. Thus a buyer with a neutral attitude could buy the analysis brand 70 per cent of the time and be included, while an extremely unfavorable buyer was included if she purchased it up to 30 per cent of the time.

The differences between the groups can be seen clearly from an overview of the mean[18] attitude scores for each group:

Group I = 1.274
Group II = 4.200
Group X = 4.218
Group Y = 1.333

Description of Explanatory Variables

The problem of developing empirical analogues to the theoretical constructs is a central issue in this analysis, just as it was with the durables analysis. In this situation we are in better shape to meet this challenge, for a number of comprehensive questions about individual behavior were included which are not usually available in studies with a specific strategic emphasis.

The variables available to this analysis are described briefly in Table 5–5. An analysis of the matrix of correlations of these variables, and tests of the stability of the discriminant coefficients in several step-wise analyses, indicated that no problems from multi-collinearity would result if the original variables were used in the discriminant analysis comparisons. In part this is because some of the variables shown in Table 5–5 are indices constructed arbitrarily from a number of other variables. (These are described fully in Appendix E: Table E–6.)

(A) ENVIRONMENTAL FACTORS

I. *Exposure to information.* Here we have to rely on inferences from three rather general variables: number of visitors, number of out-of-the-home visits, and number of hours of television viewing reported by the respondent. This environmental factor should not be expected to have nearly the same relevance as it did in the durables situation, for the product is well established, most buyers purchase it on a regular basis, and there was no unusual promotional activity during the time of the panel. Also, most of the

---

18. A score of 1 is extremely favorable; a score of 7 is extremely unfavorable.

new information will relate to changes in prices and deals, which tend to have a momentary impact on specific purchase decisions, and in any event can be dealt with more directly.

II. *Opportunity to make a brand choice.* Product availability is not really an issue in this product class because the brand we are studying, and the main competition, both have very extensive distribution. If there is any effect we would expect it to be most pronounced with the buyers who patronize small stores, in rural areas, that have limited brand offerings in all product categories. The only appropriate variable in this context is "size of city." This variable will probably not yield any important results, for it is quite removed from the phenomenon, and furthermore this type of convenience food product is not very popular in rural areas, so it will not apply to many buyers.

III. *Price and financial constraints.* Two direct measures of

Table 5–5—Independent Variable Descriptions: Non-Durables Analysis

A. *Determinants of the stability of the attitude.*
    1. Interest in the differences among brands in the product class.
    2. Confidence in judgments about brands in the product class.

B. *Determinants of "buying style."*
    3. Perceived impulsiveness in buying.
    4. Economy consciousness.
    5. Perceived time pressure.

C. *Demand, price, and store response variables.*
    6. Total number of units purchased.
    7. Average price paid per unit.
    8. Range from highest to lowest price paid.
    9. Dealing dummy variable (0=no purchases on deal).
    10. Store activity dummy variable (0=all purchases of product made in one store).

D. *Exposure to information.*
    11. Number of visitors to house.
    12. Number of invitations to visit friends.
    13. Television viewing (hours per week by respondent).

E. *Socioeconomic and demographic variables.*
    14. Size of city.
    15. Size of household.
    16. Age of housewife.
    17. Presence of children.
    18. Education of housewife.
    19. Occupation of head of household.
    20. Household income.
    21. Hours housewife employed.

the effect of price are available: average price paid per unit purchased, and the range of prices paid. As price consciousness increases (to the highest level in Criterion Group II), both the average price and the range or prices paid should decline. Buyers who are extremely price conscious would be expected to pay prices that varied within a small range, because they would exert extra effort to find the lowest price. Because this product is not a staple item, it is possible that this group would defer a purchase rather than pay a high price.

One revealing measure, which could not be directly included in the discriminant analysis because the frequency distribution was badly skewed,[19] is the percentage of total units that were purchased on some kind of deal or coupon (see Table 5–6). These results provide strong support for the hypothesis that deals act as environmental influences to make the brand more attractive to buyers in Criterion Group II (who otherwise might not buy the brand). In the discriminant comparison of Groups I and II the deal buying variable had to be treated as a dummy (0 or 1), so the results in Table 5–6 may be somewhat obscured.

IV. *Family decision processes.* Although the housewife (the panel reporter) is a user of the product in approximately 90 per cent of the households, there is the possibility that, as the size of the household increases, the housewife is more likely to consider the brand preferences of others than herself. This possibility can be evaluated with the variables reporting size of household and presence and number of children.

V. *Attraction of competing brands.* The statement made

Table 5–6—Percentage of Total Units Purchased on Deal

Criterion Group	Units on Deal (% of Total)	Average Units Purchased (Total)
I	27.0%	20.7
II	36.2	15.3
X	28.0	8.7
Y	17.2	21.3

19. More than half the buyers made no purchase on deal or by coupon.

earlier for durables applies equally well here. There is no variable available that will test this hypothesis in this context (although the competing brands can be readily defined). Second, we have assumed that the influence of competing brands is entirely inhibiting and this will not show a differential effect between Criterion Groups I and II.

(B) MODERATING EFFECTS

I. *Buying style.* As a review of Table 5–5 will show, the theoretical constructs discussed in Chapter 3 are well represented in this study. The only construct not specifically measured is the desire to change the on-going purchase pattern by trying different alternatives. To some extent this desire for novelty is a function of purchase volume, a variable which is available. But as we noted earlier, this variable may be moderated in turn by the buyer's tolerance for ambiguity (of which nothing is known).

II. *Attitude stability.* This moderator is adequately represented by two interrelated variables;[20] namely, confidence in ability to judge between brands and interest in the difference between brands. In appraising these variables it is important to realize that the average housewife is less interested in brand differences in this category than in other categories such as aspirin and detergents

Table 5–7—Average Interest in Differences Among Brands in Selected Product Categories

(n = 955 unless otherwise shown)

Product Category	Average Interest Score[a]
Convenience food product which included "analysis" brand	
— total sample	3.50
— users of product (n=220)	3.22
— nonusers (n=735)	3.58
Aspirin (total sample)	2.73
Detergents (total sample)	2.21

[a] This variable was scaled as follows:
 1 = extremely interested in the differences among brands.
 2 = very interested.
 3 = somewhat interested.
 4 = only slightly interested.
 5 = not interested at all.

20. The product-moment correlation is 0.63.

(see Table 5–7). To some extent however, this is because there are fewer users of this category than of the others.

III. *Extraneous determinants of response.* We are most interested in the possibility of a yea-saying response bias that colors all responses. This bias has been hypothesized to be either a consistently favorable frame of reference, or the consequence of a less structured and less definite attitude.

A number of measures that might capture the presence of a yea-saying response were explored. One such variable was the degree of correspondence between the position on the general "affect" scale, and the position on each of the twelve attribute evaluation scales for the analysis brand. Unfortunately this measure was badly contaminated by "halo" effects, if in fact it did reflect an acquiesence set.

Finally it was decided that the response bias would only create significant problems if it led to significant misclassification of buyers between Criterion Groups I and II. In other words, was Criterion Group I inflated in size relative to Group II? To test this hypothesis we used attitudes of the buyers in these two groups toward two brands of moderately similar products. If yea-saying biases did cause misclassification we would expect the group mean attitudes for all three brands to be significantly different. Instead, in Table 5–8 we see that, as the product becomes less and less similar to the one under study, that the difference between group means almost disappears. Presumably if group mean brand attitude scores were available for several unrelated products there would be no discernable differences. Of course all this analysis

Table 5–8—Evidence for the Presence of an Acquiesence Set in Attitudes Toward the Non-Durables Analysis Brand

| Brand | ATTITUDE OF BUYERS OF ANALYSIS BRAND | |
	Initially Favorable (Criterion Group I)	Initially Unfavorable or Neutral (Criterion Group II)
1. Analysis brand	1.287	4.208
2. Major brand of product (A) quite similar to product under study	2.445	2.948
3. Major brand of a less similar product (B)	1.778	1.987

tells us is that we don't have to worry about misclassification. The more complex problem of bias entirely within a criterion group requires a measure of overall agreement tendency based on a large number of items.

Results from the Testing Procedure

Here we will follow the order of tests outlined earlier in the chapter.

DIFFERENCES IN SEGMENT RESPONSE CHARACTERISTICS

The segment dimensions were chosen from the two largest beta coefficients in a multiple regression equation with the residual of the attitude–behavior relationship as dependent variable and the independent variables from Table 5–5. The coefficients in the following are in beta form:[21]

$$u_i = 2.62 + 0.166X_{20} + 0.165X_2 + 0.161X_{10} +$$
$$0.155X_7 + 0.110X_{11} + 0.105X_{14}$$

$$R^2 = 0.153 \quad F(21,190) = 1.60 \quad \text{Significant } p < 0.05$$

According to this result the two variables which account for the largest amount of variability in response to environmental influences are household income (X_{20}) and confidence in judgments about brands in the product class (X_2). These two variables were combined to define six segment groups.

Several interesting patterns emerge when the attitude–subsequent behavior relationship is estimated separately for each segment group. The results are summarized in Table 5–9 and Figure 5–3. If we look at the extreme groups, which are 1 (high confidence—high income) and 5 (low confidence—high income), the differences in the *slopes* (β of 14.4 versus 4.7) and in the *dispersion* (R^2 of 0.540 versus 0.041) are startling. These results are clearly not due to differences in the reliability of the purchase probability measures, because the extreme groups were almost identical in the average number of units purchased.

---

21. The beta coefficients of the other variables in the table 5–5 were not significant.

The income variable plays an interesting role as an *intensifier* of the differences between groups. This can be seen from a separate analysis, when confidence was used alone as the basis for classifying the sample into segment groups. Then the spread in R^2 (adj) between the high and low confidence groups was 0.454 to 0.125; which means the dispersion differs by a factor of 13.2 when income is included and only 3.6 when it is not included. Apparently income is a proxy for a more basic moderator, perhaps relating to buying style. On the other hand it could also represent another dimension of confidence, by establishing expectations regarding ability to make judgments. One might hypothesize that high income people have high expectation about their ability or expertise and become very uncertain when these expectations are not met.

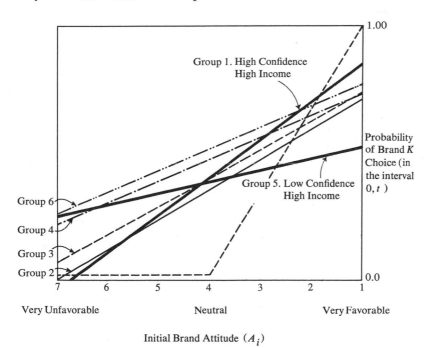

Figure 5–3. **The effect of segmentation on the predictive value of brand attitudes.**

(See Table 5–9 for definition of groups.)

139

Table 5-9—Comparison of Segment Groups

Group	Size of Group	MEANS OF CLASSIFICATION		r^2 Adjusted	Coefficients	MEAN VALUES		
		Confidence in Judgments	Income			Attitude (A_i)	Behavior $P\{K|P\}_{ji}$	Number of Units Purchased
1	25	High	High	.540[a]	$P\{K|P\}_{ji} = 83.0 - 14.4A_i$ (2.8)	2.52	.611	15.0
2	28	High	Low	.415[a]	$P\{K|P\}_{ji} = 70.9 - 11.8A_i$ (2.7)	2.60	.518	22.8
3	56	Medium	High	.225[a]	$P\{K|P\}_{ji} = 71.6 - 11.0A_i$ (2.8)	3.27	.467	10.3
4	47	Medium	Low	.192[a]	$P\{K|P\}_{ji} = 71.0 - 8.1A_i$ (2.5)	2.46	.591	18.5
5	29	Low	High	.041	$P\{K|P\}_{ji} = 51.9 - 4.7A_i$ (4.4)	3.55	.399	14.3
6	35	Low	Low	.245[a]	$P\{K|P\}_{ji} = 77.0 - 8.8A_i$ (2.7)	3.45	.553	15.5
Total sample	220	—	—	.242	$P\{K|P\}_{ji} = 71.6 - 9.8A_i$ (1.16)	3.00	.519	15.0

[a] Significant $P < .005$.

140

From Table 5–10 it can be seen that there is a big difference in the probability of purchase between the two extreme groups. For these two groups, at least, it appears that brand loyalty and the predictive value of brand attitudes are related. This implication will be explored in detail in Chapter 6.

COMPARISON ONE

Here we look in detail at the most basic group difference: buyers who like the brand and buy it versus those who are neutral or dislike the brand, but buy it nonetheless. Because we do not utilize the information on the probability of brand choice, the analysis is identical to the one used with the durables data. After combining criterion groups I and Y there are 103 buyers who like

Table 5–10—Comparison one: Buyers Favoring the Non-Durables Analysis Brand versus Buyers who are Neutral or Dislike the Brand

Description of Variable	Standardized Discriminant Coefficients (ranked in descending order)
1. Average price paid per unit	1.000
2. Household size	0.891
3. Age of housewife	0.562
4. Confidence in brand judgments	0.530
5. Television viewing	0.435
6. Impulsiveness in buying	0.420
7. Time pressure	0.418
8. Number of children	−0.390
9. Education of housewife	0.368
10. Invitations to visit	0.352
11. Range of prices paid	0.280

STATISTICAL TESTS

Mahalanobis $D^2 = 53.35$ Significance: $P < 0.001$
Efficiency of classification

		Predicted Group Membership		
		I + Y	II + X	
Actual Group Membership	I + Y	68	35	103
	II + X	18	49	67
	Total	86	84	170

Percentage correct hits
(1) Discriminant function = 69.0%
(2) Chance = 51.2

Improvement = 17.8%

the brand. This leaves 67 buyers who are neutral or dislike the brand. The average attitude of the first group is 1.29, while the average for the second is 4.21.

The results are very much as expected, with the environmental factors of price and household size dominating the comparison. Specifically, the results show that buyers who bought the brand but didn't initially like it tend to (1) pay a lower price (and as we saw earlier to make more purchases of the product on a deal), (2) come from larger households, and (3) watch more television. Perhaps as a consequence of the larger average household size, the average age in Criterion Group II is somewhat younger and the households have more children. With the exception of confidence in brand judgments the moderating effects played a minor role. The presence of

Table 5-11—Comparison Two: Influence of Environmental Factors on the Criterion Groups that are Consistent with the Model

Description of Variables	Standardized Discriminant Coefficients (ranked in descending order)
1. Average price paid per unit	1.000
2. Household size	0.860
3. Television viewing	0.592
4. Age of housewife	0.570
5. Confidence in brand judgments	0.570
6. Number of children	0.500
7. Time pressure	0.455
8. Impulsiveness	0.420
9. Education of housewife	0.362
10. Income	0.288

STATISTICAL TESTS

Mahalanobis $D^2 = 41.84$ Significance: $P < 0.005$
Efficiency of classification

		Predicted Group Membership		
		I	II	
Actual Group Membership	I	60	24	84
	II	10	33	43
Total		70	57	127

Percentage of correct hits
(1) Discriminant function = 73.5%
(2) Chance = 54.0

Improvement = 19.5%

confidence as a discriminator between the groups (although only half as influential as price for example) should not be too surprising given the key role this variable played in identifying homogeneous response segments. Any comments are somewhat premature, as this analysis included those groups of buyers who over-reacted to the environment and therefore demonstrated an inconsistent response pattern.

COMPARISON TWO

Here we will look only at Groups I and II, where the influence of environmental factors should be more pronounced (see Table 5–11). The elimination of the inconsistent group of buyers of the brand has sharpened the role of the environmental factors. It is

Table 5–12—Simultaneous Five-way Comparison of Four Criterion Groups of Buyers Plus the Non-Buyers of a Non-Durables Analysis Brand

(A) Normalized Classification Matrix[a]

		PREDICTED GROUP MEMBERSHIP				
		II	X	Y	Non-Buyers	Total
	I	.42	.15	.12	.19	.12	1.00
Actual Group	II	.09	.35	.16	.14	.26	1.00
Membership	X	.17	.17	.38	.11	.17	1.00
	Y	.16	.17	.21	.53	.05	1.00
Non-buyers		.15	.12	.20	.07	.46	1.00

(B) Association Diagram[b]

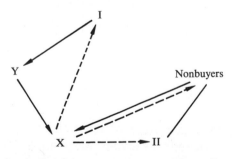

a The discriminant function classified 41.8 per cent correctly, whereas the chance level was 25.8 per cent hits.

Mahalanobis $D^2 = 123.09$ Significance < 0.001 level

b Dotted lines mean a tie.

obvious, however, that the consistent groups as defined arbitrarily here, are not homogeneous in attitude stability, or in buying style. Yet even with the loose definition imposed here, it is important to note that the main difference between Criterion Groups I and II lies in the facilitating role of the environment.

COMPARISON THREE

The next question is whether the consistent groups are in fact different from the inconsistent groups and the non-buyers of the brand (see Table 5–12). This comparision is an elaboration on the first test (in which the residual u_i was used as the dependent variable), that allows us to look at the patterns of similarity and dissimilarity between individual criterion groups, after considering all the explanatory variables. In the association diagram used to summarize the overall classification matrix, the arrows indicate the direction of misclassification for the single largest off-diagonal entry in each row of the matrix.

These results provide one more thread of evidence in support of the basic model. Despite one or two ambiguities the results are very much as we would expect on an *a priori* basis: (1) Criterion Group II is most like the non-buyer category, because if it were not for the facilitating effects of the environment Criterion Group II would remain non-buyers of the brand. (2) Similarly, Group X is most like Group II and the non-buyer group, as it differs largely in the extent of reaction to the environment. (3) Finally, there is limited evidence that Group Y is like Group I, which is reasonable because both groups were inhibited by the environment.

Summary

This empirical exploration of the influences on the form and strength of the attitude–behavior relationship has supported the theoretical model from two directions.

The most effective demonstration has come from the opportunity to array groups of buyers along a continuum of brand attitudes, with attitudes toward brands of expensive appliances at one end, and the other end being brands of a non-durables product where the buyer has highly stable judgments about the brand. In moving from one end of the continuum to the other (as attitudes become more stable, the repurchase cycle shortens and the importance of an individual purchase tends to decline) the form of the attitude–behavior relationship shifted down from the horizontal toward the 45 degree line of isomorphism between attitudes and behavior. In effect attitudes became better predictors of brand choice behavior, and in terms of the model they became better predictors because the environmental factors had much less impact on the individual choice decision.

The direct search for the facilitating and inhibiting effects of the environment was successful to the extent that suitable variables were available to describe the environment the buyer encountered. The greatest success, with both durables and non-durables products, was in uncovering the hypothesized effects of price and economic constraints. By contrast, the greatest problems were encountered with the determinants of information exposure, and in one case the results using this variable were contrary to expectations because of various inadequacies of the measure. With this one exception, however, the results were entirely consistent with the theory and strongly supportive.

Chapter 6

An Overview: With Some Implications for Marketing Strategy and Further Research

In this chapter we want to look beyond the results of the empirical tests and the theoretical groundwork. Now that a model has been developed which is a satisfactory representation of the attitude–behavior relationship, it is time to see if it has value for ongoing problems of marketing strategy and as a guide to further research and theoretical development. To put this discussion in the proper context it is necessary to retrace the steps that have been taken to this point.

Evaluating the Theoretical Structure

From a review of earlier work on the predictive relationship of attitudes and behavior certain standards were developed which served as the goals of this study. Specifically, adequate understanding of the relationship was seen to require the separation of attitudes and behavior (or behavior sequences) by significant time periods to avoid the limitations of one-time recall of behavior; understanding also required some estimate of the form and strength of the relationship at the level of individual responses; and, most important of all, adequate understanding dictated the specification and identification of the influences on the relationship.

These requirements have been organized within a model extensively adapted from learning theory and the latent structure concept of attitudes. From a single latent structure we elicit a brand attitude as the verbal representation (with all the imperfections this implies) and observe brand choice behavior over a period of time as the behavioral manifestation. With these two variables alone the shape, elevation, and strength of the predictive relationship can be estimated. To look behind this relationship and explain the observed shape, a variety of environmental factors, which influence the behavioral manifestation of the latent structure, must be considered. Because of such environmental factors as price, financial constraints, family decision processes, new information, and lack of availability, it was shown that the behavior would be dampened, and hence never be as extreme as the attitude. Because this damping takes place over a lengthy period of time, and leads to either a momentary or permanent change in the latent structure, the environmental factors can be treated as stimuli in a learning framework. This is not the whole story, for it is well known that similar attitudes conceal wide individual differences in the motive strength of the latent structure. These differences in turn lead to different reactions to environmental factors, and are often accompanied by tendencies to buy on impulse, and contamination from response biases. To handle these complexities it is necessary to incorporate moderating effects into the model to explain the *strength* of the observed relationship (which depends on the extent of inconsistent, or error producing behavior).

Testing the model

The burden of Chapter 5 was to show that the model could be accommodated to different kinds of purchase decisions, ranging from appliances to convenience foods, and properly reflect many of the multiple influences on the relationship. This was encouraging, coming as it did after a demonstration that the underlying assumptions used to define the attitude–behavior relationship were correct, that is, that the relationship is monotonic, that a single measure of affect contains most of the predictive information in brand attitudes, that attitudes have less predictive value for products with long repurchase cycles (as expected because of the increasing influences of the environmental factors), and that environmental factors do exert a damping effect as predicted.

Some reflections on the problems of empirically testing a general buyer behavior model may be helpful at this point. First, we have found that no general model can be applied directly to a specific product situation without very sensitive adaptation that takes into account various peculiarities of the market and the brands being studied. The most notable problem was the ineffectiveness of some empirical counterparts to theoretical constructs, because they were too general in nature. What is needed are explanatory variables that tap a single theoretical construct, and yet are obviously related to the brand, the product, or the product decision, as the case may be. The failure of the hypothesis about exposure to new information in the durables context is due in part to the use of variables that applied to all kinds of buying decisions, including food and drugs, and not just to durable goods. Better still would have been a report of what actually happened at the time of decision, or in several similar decisions.

More detailed findings that raise interesting issues, or call existing theory into question are

The question of just how buyers respond to information—given that durables buyers, who bought a brand they didn't initially like, *seem* to be less interested in, or desirous of obtaining information. (This whole question is confused by the inadequacy of the measures discussed above.)

The *seeming* relevance of the extraneous determinants of response (and the difficulty of measuring them) make this a fruitful area of study. This whole question is beclouded by the relationship of extraneous determinants to the firmness of the attitude and the very tentative conclusion that they seem to be less important for non-durables than for durables.

Income was found to have an important moderating effect, even though it (along with confidence) did not account for a great deal of the variability in the residual of the attitude–behavior relationship. It is not at all obvious just what role income is playing here, but the answer could have considerable significance.

Some Marketing Implications

We have already reviewed some of the possible ways that marketing strategists can profit from the application of this model to stable product environments (see the end of Chapter 2). Generally these have very direct implications for the structure of specific markets and the sources of sales for individual brands. What we are interested in discussing here are a variety of general findings that may be useful in all product categories that are dominated by nationally distributed and differentiated brands.

Market Segmentation

The most specific finding in this study was the tracing of a good deal of the unimpressive predictive performance of brand attitudes to one or two market segments—defined jointly by confidence in brand judgments and income. Within these unstable segments inter-brand differences are virtually meaningless, and each brand choice is apparently based on the environmental situation at the time of purchase.

Prior knowledge of the size of the unstable segment(s) can add considerable precision to current techniques for measuring advertising effectiveness and brand switching behavior. The general approach would be to analyze the unstable groups separately, because their attitudes will appear to be much easier to change and, as a consequence, their behavior is likely to seem erratic by comparison with other buyers. If these groups are not removed, any over-time measure of change is likely to be badly distorted and overstated. For example, if the unstable segment

149

constitutes most of the change observed in an advertising effectiveness study the results probably mean much less in terms of increased sales than would the corresponding amount of change in the stable segments. Similarly, it is desirable to look at unstable segments separately when drawing implications from transition matrices designed to measure brand switching. Because the behavior of buyers in this group is so much more erratic, and likely to be governed by momentary decisions, the transition matrix would contain large margins of error and accordingly produce very unreliable diagnoses and projections. These comments all relate to the need for more sensitive and informed use of the techniques. They should not be construed as suggesting that the information about the unstable segments is valueless. On the contrary, knowledge of the size of these segments vis-à-vis the rest of the market can say a great deal about the nature of the market, and certainly a marketing manager could learn a great deal about the strength of his brand from the proportion of sales he draws from this group. This leads us toward a discussion of brand loyalty, where the confidence in brand judgments variable functions in concert with other explanatory variables to provide some useful insights into this elusive concept.

Brand Loyalty as a Two-Dimensional Concept

There is wide agreement that the current one-dimensional or behavioristic definitions of brand loyalty (that is, based only on sequences of purchases) have contributed relatively little understanding, beyond demonstrating that brand choice decisions are not wholly random. The problem seems to lie in the inability of these definitions to produce clear-cut and useful distinctions between groups of buyers. This view has been bluntly stated by Frank after a review of the current state of empirical research:

> Brand loyal customers almost completely lack identifiability in terms of either socioeconomic or personality characteristics . . . Loyal customers do not appear to have economically important differences in their sensitivity to

either the short-run effects of pricing, dealing, and retail advertising, or to the introduction of new brands.[1]

The reasons for the comparative sterility of work on this problem are not entirely clear. One intuitively doubts that loyalty is as nebulous or even illusory as it now appears. But certainly we won't know otherwise by persisting to use arbitrary and inflexible definitions that overlook the nature of the market and the buyer's "attachment"[2] to the brand. By so doing we are assuming that there are no unique reasons for loyalty within specific markets, and also that all buyers with the same loyalty "score" are homogeneous. This last assumption is particularly questionable in view of the sizeable amount of inconsistent behavior observed in the buying of the non-durables product. Many of these buyers would conventionally be called loyal, when in actual fact their behavior is the result of a series of expedient, perhaps even random, decisions. The greater the proportion of these kinds of buyers included in the loyal group the more spurious the loyalty measures and the harder loyalty is to identify.

One solution to the limitations observed above is to have a brand loyalty score that is brand specific and positively related to the attitude toward the brand, as follows:

$$L_i = \frac{P[B_i]}{kA_i^n} = f(X_a, X_b, \ldots X_j)$$

where:

L_i = the brand loyalty score for the ith buyer of brand m,

$P[B]_i$ = proportion of total purchases of the product that buyers devoted to brand m over the period of the study,

A_i = the attitude toward brand m at the beginning of the study (scaled so that a low value represents a favorable attitude),

---

1. Frank (1967, page 33).
2. A similar point has been made by Newman (1966). See Chapter 2.

Table 6-1—Effect of Changes in Brand Loyalty Measure and Descriptive Variables on Regression Results

Equation Number	Weighting Scheme for $L_i = P[B_i] \div kA|_i$	Descriptive Variables			
		(A) SOCIOECONOMIC AND DEMOGRAPHIC ONLY		(B) ALL DESCRIPTIVE VARIABLES	
		R^2 Adjusted	Standard Error of Estimate	R^2 (Adjusted)	Standard Error of Estimate
1	$k = 1$; $n = 0$ [Usual measure of brand loyalty]	0.035	28.70	0.158	28.05
2	$k = 1$; $n = 1$	0.068	33.65	0.270[a]	30.60
3	$k = 1/2$; $n = 1$	0.068	67.23	0.270[a]	61.20
4	$k = 2$; $n = 1$	0.053	18.09	0.221[b]	17.08
5	$k = 1$; $n = 1/2$	0.052	30.01	0.232[b]	28.59

a = Significant at < 0.01 level   b = Significant at < 0.05 level.

$X_a, X_b, .. X_j$ = descriptive variables to be fitted to L_i by least squares (these are described in Table 5–5),

k, n = constants whose values are varied by trial and error to maximize the fit between L_i and $X_a, X_b, ... X_j$.

This approach is not without problems. Basically, it is not obvious what weights should be given the relative influence of the attitude and behavior components in the loyalty score. For lack of a better criteria it is assumed here that the weights are defined by the best fit between the loyalty score (described above) and the descriptive variables used in the multiple regression equation. There are also the problems we have encountered before, of combining a one-time attitude measure and an over-time measure of behavior.

The data in Table 6–1 are based on the non-durables results that were analyzed in Chapter 5. The results are a summary of a series of multiple regression equations in which various weights for the continuous brand loyalty score (L_i) were fitted to two different sets of descriptive variables.

The key results are found in the contrast (a) between equations 1(A) and 1(B) in which the additional descriptive variables raised the R^2 from 0.036 to 0.158 when the usual measure of brand loyalty was used, and (b) between equations 1(B) and 3(B) in which the two-dimensional measure of brand loyalty raised the R^2 from 0.158 to 0.270 when the full set of descriptive variables was used.

Describing true brand loyal buyers. The next step was to identify the specific variables that contribute the most to the description. The relative contribution of each variable (expressed as a Beta coefficient) in equation 2(B) is summarized in Table 6–2. The results provide a reasonably consistent picture of the true brand loyal buyer as:

Very conscious of the need to economize when buying.
Confident of her brand judgements.
A heavy buyer of the product.

153

An older housewife in a smaller than average size household (who therefore needs to satisfy the preferences of fewer family members).

Apparently less influenced by day-to-day price fluctuations, as evidenced by the fact that, although the price paid per unit is close to average, the range of prices is quite narrow and fewer purchases tended to be made on deal.

Other less significant findings, which help to focus the picture of the true brand loyal buyer, indicate that these buyers are less impulsive and patronize fewer stores. There is some evidence that these buyers also have less exposure to personal sources of information (at least through visits to friends). Nothing conclusive can be said about media exposure because of the gross nature of the variable used.

A plausible interpretation of the description above is that true

Table 6–2—Describing Two-Dimensional Brand Loyalty Scores
(Coefficients are for Equation 2B=Table 6–1)

Variable	Ranked Beta Coefficients
1. Economy consciousness	−1.00a
2. Confidence in brand judgments	−0.95a
3. Household size	−0.86b
4. Total number of units purchased	0.80b
5. Range of prices paid	−0.75a
6. Presence of children	−0.64
7. Dealing	−0.63a
8. Age of housewife	−0.59b
9. Invitations to visit	−0.59a
10. Impulsiveness	0.54b
11. Store activity	−0.42

Notes:

(a) The largest Beta coefficient was set equal to 1.00 and the rest of the coefficients were scaled proportionately.

(b) The stepwise addition of the remaining ten variables lead to an increase in the standard error of estimate.

(c) Adjusted R^2 for this equation is .270 , based on a sample of 148 buyers of the brand.

(d) Below are the raw regression coefficients (with standard errors) for the above independent variables. Subscripts refer to the order in which the variables are ranked above.

$$L_i = 127.5 - 3.89X_1 - 3.52X_2 - 4.07X_3 + 0.34X_4 - 1.37X_5 - 2.05X_6$$
$$(1.28) \quad (1.55) \quad (3.46) \quad (0.15) \quad (0.79) \quad (1.75)$$
$$- 10.61X_7 - 0.29X_8 - 3.59X_9 + 2.93X_{10} - 6.51X_{11}$$
$$(5.89) \quad (0.22) \quad (2.50) \quad (1.80) \quad (5.58)$$

a = Significant at < .01 level; b = Significant at < .05 level.

brand loyal buyers are *committed* to the value and price appeal of the brand (by virtue of being confident that they have judged the brand correctly), coupled with their perceived need to economize. This interpretation is supported by an independent correlation of 0.331 ($r^2 — 0.110$) between the loyalty measure (L_i) and a semantic differential scale with opposite poles reading "good buy for the money—not a good buy for the money."

According to this study, any one or all of the following hypotheses about the nature of brand loyalty merit serious consideration: (1) Loyalty is based on a *rational* decision made after an evaluation of the benefits of competing brands. This decision is, in effect, a commitment to the brand. Such decisions are likely made on an infrequent basis, and once made, the buyer either (2) feels that such an explicit decision is no longer necessary before each purchase, in which case the process becomes *habitual*, or (3) his strong affective orientation toward the brand narrows his perceptual judgment, and he is less likely to see competitive promotional activity (Bieri, 1967). Obviously the commitment is never total, and the decision is reviewed when competitive or other circumstances change.

There is nothing in the descriptive findings of this study that contradict any of the above hypotheses. Evidence for an initial rational decision is particularly compelling, given the fact that true brand loyal buyers have the greatest degree of confidence in their ability to judge between brands. Also, we can infer that because the loyal buyers are heavier than average[3] buyers of the product, that they have more experience on which to base an explicit decision. Heavy buyers also have more to gain by adopting an habitual pattern, which will permit them to economize on the effort of

3. Average purchase volume was 20 units for the switchers, 15 units for the spuriously loyal, and 24 units for the true loyal buyers. Farley (1964) studied the competing hypotheses that heavy buyers tend to be less brand loyal because they have more to gain by searching for the lowest price or the best value. The hypothesis was generally not borne out by the data, perhaps because the theoretical requirement that consumers consider brands as good substitutes was not satisfied in all the product classes studied. This requirement was obviously not satisfied in this product class.

repeated decisions. The habit hypothesis is further supported by the finding that true brand loyal buyers tend to be older, and presumably have developed greater rigidity in their preferences. Of course, it was easier for the older buyers of this product to maintain a habitual pattern, as they typically represented small households with fewer competing preferences to consider.

The evidence for a perceptual bias against competing stimuli (whether packaging, promotion, or advertising) is tentative but very suggestive, as otherwise there would be a direct contradiction in true brand loyal buyers being economy conscious while at the same time paying prices that are close to average, fall within a narrow range, and are less likely to include a deal. There is apparent support for this hypothesis, but from a different direction, in a study recently reported by Bogart (1967, page 205), that found that the highest level of readership of advertisements of a product occurred among users who were brand loyal ,"but not among the *most* brand loyal."

A Methodology for Test Market Evaluation

Test market panels (and store audits to a lesser extent) are an irritating paradox for marketing decision makers. When such panels are used for new product introductions the question of *projectibility* looms large in decisions about the size, type, and location of the panel. Care must be taken to obtain representative samples and avoid sensitizing the behavior of the panel members. Yet most of this effort turns out to be of no avail, for test market conditions invariably differ from national market conditions, particularly if a year or two have lapsed. This problem is now well recognized and most decision makers ultimately place little weight on the panel performance as a guide to future performance, preferring to use the results for diagnostic purposes. This being the case, Stanton asks some revealing questions about the way test panels and test markets should be designed and put to use,

What would happen if researchers recognized [the] limitations of test marketing and blatantly stated that test-market results for new products are not projectible?

Suppose they put aside the fear of disrupting the share-of-market reading

156

and engaged in extraordinary research inquiries or even the testing of radical new marketing approaches during the test market period. Suppose that researchers abandoned entirely the aim of calibrating the precise levels of consumer acceptance of the new brand, and substituted for it the objective of using the test market to exploit fully the brand's profit and volume potentials.[4]

The panel methodology used in the non-durables analysis, and to some extent in the durables analysis, is admirably suited to the kinds of investigations that Stanton foresees. Granted, the long battery of attitude and classification quizzes prior to the beginning of the panel did bias the share of the analysis brand upward. More important however, these additional manipulations did *not* appear to affect basic relationships (see Appendix C for the supporting evidence). Once the need for projectibility is removed this becomes the important consideration. As long as the proportions can safely be assumed to be stable, then the addition of attitudinal and other variables to the basic panel design offers a wealth of opportunities to learn about the source of trial and repeat sales, the nature and permanence of the core of heavy buyers, the effect of the new product on contiguous markets or competing company brands, the reasons for the observed substitution or complementarity effects, the effect of novelty appeals on the trial rate, the product attributes that have the greatest influence on trial and repeat, and many more. All of these questions are asked of the separate cross-section attitude surveys and independent diary panels set up to monitor the new product. But too often the inability of the research design to relate attitudes and types of people to the source of sales means the answers are not forthcoming or must be squeezed out of the data by making a series of dubious assumptions.

Directions for Further Research

This attempt to ask a series of searching theoretical and empirical questions about the attitude–behavior relationship has, if nothing

---

4. Stanton (1967, page 45).

else, succeeded in raising more questions. This is the nature of research, but the fact that there are so many unanswered questions reflects adversely on the quality of the available inputs—be they theory, the measures, or the analytical techniques. But only by building on the knowledge of past inadequacies can future progress be made.

Under ideal circumstances, the program of research required to overcome just the limitations encountered in this report should be designed to include

More products, encompassing a wider range of buying decisions (but with emphasis on those where a probability measure of behavior can be estimated).

Improved attitude scales, for example asymmetrical scales that reduce bunching of respondents in categories, to increase measurement sensitivity and the precision with which criterion groups can be identified.

More vigorous attempts to reduce respondent sensitization toward the analysis brand. This requires attitude measures toward all major brands in the market, an inconvenience that is offset by the possibility of evaluating brand interaction patterns.

Larger samples of buyers, preferably in excess of 1000 respondents. This would reduce estimation error and permit the application of programs (such as Automatic Interaction Detector) which can search out the interaction patterns which have only been partially identified in this report. With samples of this size it would also be possible to analyze more finely partitioned criterion groups. For example, instead of dichotomizing the buyers who were consistent with the model into those who were inhibited and those who were facilitated, it would be more revealing to consider separately those buyers who were close to λ, that is, not influenced strongly by the environmental factors.

Explanatory variables that have been more carefully tailored to the theoretical constructs, while maintaining a close link with the realities and idiosyncrasies of the products and brands being studied. Variables that are overly general in scope become amorphous and indistinguishable between criterion groups and may obscure important differences.

For the sake of completeness we re-emphasize that the theoretical constructs themselves leave much to be desired.

Improved Brand Attitude Scales

If explanatory variables can be improved by sensitive tailoring to the realities of the problem being studied, it follows that attitude

158

scales can be similarly improved if they are adapted to the specific problem of brand attitudes. The proliferation of scales for measuring brand attitudes is in part a recognition of this fact. One feels, however, that differences between types of brand attitude scales mostly reflect the experience or personal predilection of the researcher or the dictates of the moment. Seldom are the differences justified either theoretically or empirically (although Appendix D reviews some useful work, such as Abrams, 1966).

A generally useful scale for measuring brand attitudes is not always necessary or desirable. However, the study reported here is one instance where this kind of scale would be highly useful, particularly given some of the limitations that plague the semantic differential and Thurstone scales when they are applied to the subtle differences among brands. Before suggesting an improved general scale let us rephrase the various observed limitations into a statement of the *objectives* that should be sought by such a scale:

1. To obtain preference levels that have strategic meaning; that is, to show the source and stability of a brand's strength and, it is hoped, to reveal the effort necessary to strengthen a brand further.
2. To combine evaluation *plus* the respondent's judgment of the realities of the market (without creating two-dimensional statements). The respondent should have more explicit standards for the comparison of the various brands in the market.
3. To reflect the usual situation in most markets where brands are more or less favorably evaluated and seldom unfavorably evaluated.
4. To satisfy the usual measurement objectives of sensitivity, reliability, comparability of the scores of respondents, and ease of administration (at least by mail), and to reduce the possibility of an extremity set.

A scale that is believed to satisfy most of these objectives is shown in Figure 6–1. The value of each item position would be determined using Thurstone judgment procedures. Ideally the scale should be subjected to considerable validation research designed to find out if buyers actually view markets this way, if different categories are meaningfully different, and if the statements are unambiguous.

This scale is primarily designed to improve predictions of buying behavior. To function as a diagnostic device it must be comple-

Figure 6–1. Relative rating scale for brand attitudes.

(Note: To be complemented by measures of confidence in brand judgments plus scales for specific product attributes)

(1)	(2)	(3)	(4)	(5)	(6)	(7)
This brand is the best that is available.	I like this brand very much—but there's another just as good.	I like this brand —but others are better.	This brand is acceptable—but most other brands are better.	I neither like nor dislike this brand —it doesn't have any particular merits.	I don't like this brand very much —although it is not as bad as some.	I don't like this brand at all—it is one of the worst available.

Primary choice class

Secondary consideration class

Non-consideration class

mented by measures of confidence in brand judgments and scales for specific product attributes.

Extending the Model to Other Problems

Although the model used to organize the theoretical and empirical work in this study was specifically designed to account for the elicitation of a prior attitude and the prediction of measures of subsequent behavior, it need not be confined to this problem. By application to successive series of attitude interviews (X) and panel measures of behavior $(.O.O.O.O..)$, the model shows some potential for insights into other problems. These possibilities are only suggested below:

(1) *Design:* $X_1 .O.O.O.X_2$
   Problem: Are the effects of the environmental factors momentary or lasting? This involves the study of attitude change within each criterion group.
(2) *Design:* $X_1 .O.O.O.X_2 .O.O.O$
   Problem: Does a change in attitude between X_1 and X_2 lead to a change in behavior? This involves successive applications of the basic model. Changes in the slope of the attitude–behavior relationship between the two intervals would show whether the attitude *change* was supported or nullified by the environment.
(3) *Design:* $X_1 .O.O.X_2 .O.O.X_3$
   Problem: With this design it is possible to observe the effect of behavior change on attitude change.

Each one of these extensions represents as much or more work than the present study. Clearly there is a great deal to be done before the gaps in our knowledge about the brand attitude–brand choice behavior relationship are closed.

Appendices

Appendix A

Advantages and Limitations of Panels for Measuring the Attitude-Behavior Relationship

A panel has been defined as a technique for providing *continuous* information on behavior from a *relatively static group of consumers* (Boyd and Westfall, 1960, page 5). Usually this definition requires substantial qualification when it is applied to a particular set of problems. For the attitude–behavior relationship problem we are interested in short-run panels (five to six months), that do not require replacement during the period of operation. Two such panels are described in detail in Appendices B and C. While these two panels are quite different, one using personal interviews and the other using mail diaries, there are a number of general statements of advantages and limitations that apply to both.

Advantages of Panels

The overwhelming advantage is the opportunity to obtain records of actual behavior, close to the time of decision, which can be related to the initial attitude of the same buyers. The often used alternatives of combining attitude and behavior measures in one cross-sectional (recall) interview, or relating the attitudes of one group to the behavior of another group at a later time, were examined in Chapter 1 and found totally wanting. This conclusion about the superiority of the panel method, for this type of problem, is consistent with the findings on the effects of memory decay and motivated forgetting on recall responses (Granbois and Engel, 1965), and specific studies comparing reports of behavior in recall and panel studies (see Boyd and Westfall, 1960; and Sudman, 1964b). In particular, the study reported by Sudman shows that brand recall and usage measures are seriously biased in cross-section interviews.

Second, the continuing contact makes it possible to collect much more information about specific purchase than is otherwise possible. Most panels collect information about price, volume, size, store patronized, deals used, frequency (according to dates purchased), and so forth. The same opportunity exists to obtain detailed non-purchasing information, including brand attitudes, with which to classify buyers. This opportunity is seldom exploited in consumer panels because of the desire to limit contacts with the panel, and not bias subsequent behavior.

Third, the nature of the data permits more penetrating descriptive analysis. Under some circumstances the data can be used to determine the direction and extent of causality between sets of related variables. The types of improved description which are relevant to the attitude–behavior problem include (1) estimation of loyalty patterns and stability of behavior, (2) distinguishing between gross and net change, and (3) singling out those people who change, or change in unpredicted directions, and comparing them to the rest of the panel.

These advantages are not gained without some offsetting costs—not only in time and money, but in data that is inherently sensitive to many kinds of error, and hence may be misleading. We turn now to the problem of a little "panel knowledge" being potentially "dangerous."

Limitations of Panels

A prospective user of panel data may become paralyzed with inaction after contemplating all the possible sources of error and bias in the data. Yet, as we shall see shortly, many problems can be eliminated by careful design and implementation; and, failing elimination, it is often possible to determine the extent of the error or bias. Furthermore, when there is error or bias, it is often the case that aggregates and *projections* will be adversely affected, but "basic *relationships* generally remain relatively unbiased" (Kosobud and Morgan, 1964, page 2).

(A) THE SAMPLE UNIVERSE

Both cross-sectional and panel samples usually exclude transients, individuals in institutions or with the armed services, and so on. In addition, the households of illiterates and sick housewives are usually not included. For recruitment and operation by mail the problem of literacy can be quite troublesome.

(B) SAMPLE SIZE

When there is limited *a priori* evidence on the composition of the market being studied, in a cross-sectional survey, it is sometimes possible to use sequential sampling procedures. Even if the final sample is too large the cost of the excess can usually be absorbed. But the costs of carrying more panel members than necessary can be a considerable drain. This problem is most serious in test market panels where a large proportion may never try or adopt the brand being studied. In some circumstances it may be possible to eliminate groups that have a low probability or trial at the beginning or during the first few periods.

(C) INITIAL PARTICIPATION AND MORTALITY

The panel cross-section must be representative at all points in time, rather than just one point. Unfortunately the nature of panels and the demands on respondents make representativeness very difficult to achieve.

First, the refusal rates are always high—sometimes in excess of 50 per cent. (Figures on refusal rates have been collected and analyzed by Bucklin and Carman, 1967, page 15.) This means that the final sample is usually established by quota methods, rather than probability sampling. This is worrisome, for it is only possible to control the quotas with a limited number of standard demographic variables. However, it is certain that many other variables affect the decision to cooperate in a panel: the attraction of the financial incentive (which is probably related to price consciousness), the need for involvement with the outside world (probably higher for widows than for bachelors, for example), and the time available to participate (a probable influence on housewives who work or have large families). To the extent that non-probability methods are used, and variables like price consciousness cannot be controlled, the initial sample will not be representative.

Any recruitment biases are almost certain to be intensified by subsequent attrition. Attrition may be 25 to 35 per cent (see Allison, Zwick, and Brinser, 1958) in the first few periods when it is most severe. Nicosia (1965, page 235) notes that we know very little about the factors that affect attrition in marketing panels or the effect of these factors on the phenomena being studied. Studies of dropouts often show that people who are *interested* in the subject matter of a panel are more likely to remain in the panel. Bucklin and Carman (1967, page 17) argue that interest is probably the single determinant of attrition, other than natural causes and relocation. For support they show that interest is the common denominator in the descriptions of dropouts

167

found in many studies. For example dropouts have been found to be (1) more "other directed," (2) less systematic in their shopping, (3) from small families with no children (and at the same time younger and more mobile), although (4) high dropout rates have also been found among older families, which "suggest that when . . . children leave home, wives again busy themselves with outside interests and lose their interest in and need for shopping." (5) Also related is the tendency for the poorly educated to drop out. These may only be within the older families who had less opportunity to receive education, although lack of education could be related "to lack of interest, inefficient shopping, and an inability to follow directions."

(D) SENSITIZATION TO THE SUBJECT MATTER OF THE PANEL

The mere fact of membership in a panel is bound to increase the subject's awareness[1] of her actions and the environment—at least for a short time. This "sensitization" may be heightened by initial questions and subsequent reinterviews. Ehrenberg (1960) concluded from a study of new and old panels that the initial effect of membership doesn't seem to last more than one to three periods. This initial effect usually leads to stocking up, false reporting for prestige reasons, and perhaps the reporting of existing stocks. Thereafter, the novelty wears away and normal behavior is resumed. According to Stock (1960, page 236), the amount of conditioning from questioning, over and above the initial membership effect, is relatively minor when households are asked to report on the facts of their behavior. Roper (1964, page 522) has indicated that this may not be true when attitudes (toward companies) are concerned. An independent cross-section taken at the end of a two-wave reinterview panel did not confirm the attitude change found by the panel. Also, Ortengren (1957, page 442) believes there are usually fewer "don't know" and "no preference" responses among members of a multi-wave panel. In a similar vein Lazarsfeld (1953, page 516) reported that the final distribution of opinions in a panel study of voting behavior matched the distribution in a cross-section study, with the exception of fewer "don't knows." Nicosia

---

1. Webb, Campbell *et al.* (1966, page 13) have a classification of types of *reactive measurement effects* that is appropriate here:

(a) "The guinea pig effect—awareness of being tested . . . we have little basis for determining what is and what is not reactive."

(b) Role selection, "involves not so much inaccuracy, defense, or dishonesty, but rather a specialized selection from among the many 'true' selves or 'proper' behaviors available in any respondent."

(c) Measurement as a change agent, "introducing real changes in what is being measured," such as when processes leading to opinion development are initiated.

(d) Response sets. This question has been specifically addressed in Chapter 3.

(1965, page 236) finds this tendency encouraging, "since it makes a respondent a better reporter of his own actions and thoughts; indeed repeated interviewing may be the only way to get at routine behavior patterns and unconsciously enacted psychological processes."

(E) RECORDING ACCURACY

Panels conducted by personal or telephone interviews have the usual problems of accuracy associated with any interview situation. However, mail panels have some unique problems associated with record keeping where no direct controls are possible. Sudman (1964a, page 15) notes that the following difficulties might arise: "1. The record keeper is not aware that the purchase was made by another household member; 2. The record keeper is aware of the purchase but forgets to enter it in the diary; 3. The record keeper enters the purchase in the diary but errs on some detail of the purchase due to either a memory or a recording error; or 4. Deliberate falsification of the diary, either by omission of purchases or inclusion of imaginary purchases or purchase details." He went on to appraise the net effect of all these sources of error, by comparing panel data with shipment data, and found, "that frequently purchased grocery items are recorded very accurately . . . while up to half the purchases of unusual non-grocery items, such as phonograph records, may be omitted."

The common feature of these recording inaccuracies is that each contribute to *random error*. They may also contribute to *consistent* bias, but not to the same extent as the form of the diary (see Sudman, 1964a, page 17), or the response style of the reporter. In cross-section analysis it is the consistent bias that is troublesome, because random errors are assumed to be normal, independent, and with zero mean. According to Bucklin and Carman (1967, page 20) this is not the case with panel analysis, because random error looks just like true change in a turnover table, whereas consistent bias will still lead to the same responses in two time periods if there is no true change. Consequently, before much faith can be placed in a measure of change, it is necessary (1) to have some form of control group or test-retest reliability measure and (2) to be able to identify the people who have little interest in the subject and are most subject to random shifts.

(F) OTHER PROBLEMS

Two operational problems, which are always troublesome, concern the length of the reporting period and the handling of movers.

All other things being equal, the reporting period would be fairly long because of the increased cost of shorter periods. In fact periods are long for products that have long repurchase cycles. But as the purchase cycle shortens, and each purchase is relatively less important, the unreliability of memory leads to under-reporting. Shaffer (1955) also notes that short purchase periods reduce the possibility that the reporter will notice a pattern in the purchasing and consciously change behavior.

Sobol (1959, page 60) has investigated the implications of the fact that 17 per cent of the population move each year. Obviously this can create considerable attrition in long-term regional panels when people move out of the area. Sometimes it is not possible or feasible to maintain contact with a mover, even if the panel is national in scope. In either event the panel will contain increasing proportions of older people, of people who own their homes, and of people with incomes over $5000 (in 1954).

Appendix B

A Further Description of the
Durables Panel

The purpose of this Appendix is to expand on the discussion, in Chapter 4, of the survey methods and the behavior measures used in the durables panel. The description of the survey methods was provided by the General Electric Company Consumer Behavior Research Program, which designed and implemented the panel as part of the pilot test of a large-scale information system.

SAMPLE SELECTION

Two hundred and twenty householders were selected from the respondents in a large cross-section survey, completed between October and December, 1963. A probability sample was used in the large survey. Eight counties or metropolitan areas (Primary Sampling Units) from this probability sample were selected to achieve maximum possible geographic distribution of respondents. To facilitate later discussions with the interviewers regarding their reactions to the questionnaire it was decided that 80 interviews would be concentrated in the three counties of the Boston Metropolitan Area. The remaining 140 interviews were distributed among the other five counties.

"Within each county, households were selected from blocks or block equivalents by random methods at a rate which was determined by the number of interviews to be assigned and the expected completion rate (based on experience of the large initial survey). If more than three households were assigned in one block, the rate was varied whenever possible by dropping households from clusters which had more than three assigned interviews and adding households to clusters which had less than three."

INITIAL COOPERATION AND ATTRITION

One hundred and seventy-five Wave I questionnaires were completed in June–July 1964; an 80 per cent response rate. From among these 175 households, 150 Wave II questionnaires were completed in February 1965, an 86 per cent response rate. The very low refusal rate, compared to published experience (reviewed in Bucklin and Carman, 1967, page 15) is in part due to the preselection in the initial survey, which weeded out the least cooperative prospects. The wave to wave attrition rate of 14 per cent compares favorably with other panel studies. In addition, the interviewers were carefully selected, trained, and controlled to ensure maximum response. The same interviewer was used in each interview of a particular household to achieve better rapport —and reduce random error from different interviewing styles.

An analysis of the reasons for non-response in Waves I and II is revealing of some of the problems encountered in panel designs (see Table B–1). It is noteworthy that 40 per cent of the 70 non-responses were due to the unavailability of the household.

INCENTIVES

In total the respondents were interviewed three times, with each interview lasting an *average* of one hour. Most of the material was detailed and factual,

Table B–1—Explanation of Non-Response to Wave I and Wave II[a] of Durables Panel

(A) WAVE I

	Number	Percent
Refused		
Tired of surveys	5	
Husband disapproved	3	
Illness in family	3	
Too busy at present time	3	
Other	9	
	23	51%
Moved out of sample area	12	27
Respondent unavailable	9	20
Language barrier	1	2
Total	45	100%

(A) WAVE II

	Number	Percent
Refused[b]		
Husband disapproved	4	
Too busy at time of interview	8	
Gift not worth the time	4	
Other	6	
	19	76%
Household dissolved	2	8
Respondent unavailable	4	16
Total	25	100%

a Source: Company report.
b Add to 22 because 3 households gave more than one reason.

although apparently capable of holding the respondent's interest. To maximize the response rate, households were given small gifts at the completion of each interview. Before the Wave II interviews each household was sent a reminder letter, and requested to notify the interviewer of any change in address. A large gift was also offered to 105 of the 175 Wave I respondents, during the first wave, if they completed the second wave. For those promised the larger gift, refusals were slightly lower and completed interviews slightly higher in both waves.

MEMORY AND RECALL

It was expected that the aggregate number of appliances entering inventories should approximately equal the number being dropped. Yet final results showed 295 acquisitions and 151 dispositions. If this was representative it would mean that inventories were growing at an astronomical rate, when in fact they had been stable for several years. It is possible that acquisitions make more of an impact, and are remembered better than the phasing out of an unwanted, and probably unusable, appliance. Were appliances not so expensive, this disparity might represent the sensitizing effect of the panel. According to analyses by General Electric the explanation is that the Wave II interviews came shortly after the Christmas gift buying season, so that (1) the six months acquisitions were in fact more than 70 per cent of total annual acquisitions, and (2) the respondent could remember the acquisition of even the smallest houseware appliance because of the recency of the event. This explanation has some interesting implications for the timing and interval of recall interviews, but at the least it suggests that the purchase data are reliable.

MEASURES USED IN THE ATTITUDE–BEHAVIOR STUDY

The attitude measure is described in detail in Appendix D. The behavior measure deserves some comment here. First, most of the analysis was done with a "composite" brand, that was actually an aggregate of seven very different, nationally distributed, full-line brands. It was noted in Chapter 4 that this conceals differences due to the nature of better-known versus lesser-known brands, and between manufacturer versus distributor-controlled brands (such as Sears and Wards). Second, a further aggregation brought together expensive and less expensive types of appliances in the three categories of majors, electronics, and housewares. Some effects of this lumping together of unlike products were demonstrated in Chapter 4 for two different price categories (see Table 4–2). Even where there is little price variation it is entirely possible that a respondent may have a different attitude towards one brand, depending on whether the product is a vacuum cleaner or a black-and-white portable television set. The distortions resulting from this aggregation will only be known when further tests are made with much larger samples.

The only acquisitions considered for study were those that could be influenced by prior brand attitudes. Accordingly 43 of a total of 237 acquisitions were deleted because someone outside the household *probably* chose the brand, for example, gifts from outside the home, and appliances bought with a new house or supplied by the apartment building owner. Gifts given within the home were retained for the analysis, although there was some possibility that the reporter for the household did not choose the brand given, and might even have disliked that brand. Table B–2 shows that this effect would be most likely to influence the attitude–behavior relationship for inexpensive (that is, houseware) appliances. This possibility is examined in Chapter 5, as an environmental factor.

Unfortunately it was not possible to use a brand intentions measure, to compare with the brand attitude measure, as a predictor. Only 79 of the 150 households thought at the time of Wave I that there was at least a "good possibility" of acquiring any appliance in the following six months, and were asked which brand they intended to buy. Forty-two of these households fulfilled one or more of these buying plans, and in only 19 cases was the brand intention fulfilled. Most of the acquisitions (79 per cent) were unplanned, making brand intentions much too limited in scope compared to brand attitudes.

Table B–2—How Different Types of Appliances Were Obtained
(Percentages on column totals)

How obtained	Total	TYPE OF APPLIANCES		
		Majors	Electronics	Houseware
Bought separately	38%	65%	37%	31%
Bought with house	2	16	—	—
Supplied by building owner	a	3	—	—
Gift given within home	27	10	33	29
Gift received from outside home	15	—	17	17
Gift given outside home	16	—	11	22
Other	2	6	2	1
Total	100%	100%	100%	100%
Number of cases	237	31	66	140

a = Less than 0.5 percent.

Appendix C

A Further Description of the
Non-Durables Panel

The kind of data collected from this panel has already been described in Chapter 4. However, insufficient detail was provided about the basic features of the panel to permit an appraisal of the representativeness of the results.

For the purposes of this appendix the panel used for the analysis in this report will be called the "Columbia" panel. The parallel panel, used to appraise the effects of the various instruments, will be called the "Control" panel. Because the data were collected during a recent test market of a new convenience food product, and hence might have competitive value, all brand and product class names will be disguised, and any data that bear on market share (such as number of households buying) will be presented as the difference between the "Columbia" and the "Control" panel. However, it should be emphasized that the product class being used here for the analysis of the attitude–behavior relationship is only moderately related to the product class in which the test brand was entered.

SAMPLE SELECTION

Both panels were operated in the statewide region where the new brand was being tested. The first step in the selection of the sample was to draw at random 70,000 households from all the telephone directories in the region. In order to obtain dispersion throughout the region 70 clusters, of 1000 households each, were drawn at regular sampling intervals. Because the counties were ranked in order of descending size, the larger counties were sampled first and contained as many as 20 clusters, while some of the smaller counties did not fall into any cluster.

The next step was the mailing of a recruitment letter and a "classification quiz" to each of the selected households. The letter described the work of a panel member in interesting terms, and emphasized how helpful and necessary the information would be, but an incentive was mentioned only in passing. In fact it had been decided to award panel members with various pieces of a kitchen utensil set as they continued to participate. By de-emphasizing the incentive it was hoped that the responses would not be over-weighted in favor of "money" or "price" conscious respondents who might reflect this bias in their brand choice behavior.

Over 8000 households responded to the recruitment letter by returning the "classification quiz." This quiz provided standard demographic and recent product usage information for subsequent analysis. The response rate of 11.4 per cent compares well with mailed questionnaires in general, but of course is much poorer than the kind of response obtained by personal interview recruitment. The big advantage of mail recruitment is the much lower cost. The drawbacks are that the sample is in one sense "self-selected," and tends to be over-represented with better educated housewives. The extent of this lack of representativeness is being explored as another aspect of the Buyer Behavior Research Project.

Two matched panels of 1100 households each were selected from the overall pool of 8000 responses; one becoming the "Columbia" panel, the other the "Control" panel. The selection of the two panels was not entirely random. It had been previously decided that there would be 50 per cent more users (of the product class in which the new brand was entered) in the panel than in the population. Because present users of the product were expected to be the main source of the triers and repeaters of the new brand, the decision to over-represent users was really an attempt to increase the analysis base. To some extent this probably also meant that there would be more users of the product being analyzed in this report, because the two products were sometimes used simultaneously in the same household. Of course this modification of the sample would have no effect on the relationships being studied, although it would have to be taken into account in any projections of the results.

Before discussing cooperation and attrition it is useful to review the sequence of contacts with the "Columbia" panel. It had been assumed that the extra work load of one mail questionnaire and three telephone interviews, plus additions to the diary form, would increase the dropout rate in the "Columbia" panel over the usual rate, as represented by the "Control" panel. However there was no relevant previous experience available that would give any insights into this problem.

SEQUENCE AND TIMING OF CONTACTS

(After the respondent had been assigned to the "Columbia" panel).

(1) Week 1—An eighteen page *mail questionnaire* was sent to 1100 households and returned by 955 households. The excellent response rate, of 86.8

per cent, was attributed to the interesting nature of the questionnaire, and the fact that a gift was sent to each household, regardless of whether the questionnaire had been returned.

(2) Week 2 to Week 21—Every two weeks, during this five month period, each household sent in a purchase diary, reporting the details of purchases in five major food product categories. Only three of the five products were of interest, the other two served as disguises. Each diary included a series of general questions designed to identify the first time the household became aware of any new brand in the five product categories, the source of the awareness, the reason for the first purchase of the brand, and satisfaction in the event of usage.

(3) Week 6—*First telephone interview* (860 interviews completed). The sequence of telephone interviews was primarily designed to measure changes in awareness and attitudes toward the test brand. The switch from mail to telephone was dictated by (1) the need to compress all interviews into the shortest possible time, so individual responses were comparable, and (2) to qualify people as either aware or not-aware of the test brand, and several other brands, before asking further questions. In this way it was hoped that the interviews would not serve as a source of information toward the test brand.

Each telephone interview asked a series of questions about sources of information concerning the new brand, as well as other brands, and attitudes and intentions toward these brands. However, when a brand was not of central importance to the study it would be included only once in the first two interviews. This is the case with the brand being studied in this report, so there is some possibility that the panel members were sensitized to the brand from this source, as well as from the mail questionnaire.

(4) Week 11—*Second telephone interview* (760 interviews completed). The drop in the number of completions was due less to refusals and/or panel dropouts, than to moves out of the test market region and vacationing households putting respondents out of reach.

(5) Week 22—*Third telephone interview* (730 interviews completed). This interview came immediately after the wrap-up of the diary panel. Refusals were the highest in this interview, because some respondents thought their participation was finished and others felt that three rather dull interviews were too much of an imposition when there had been no explicit warning of any interviews at the beginning of the panel.

INITIAL COOPERATION AND ATTRITION

One criterion of attrition, which permits comparisons of the "Columbia" panel with the "Control" panel, or any other panel, is the number of households returning diaries. This figure tends to be unstable, within any particular two week period, as diaries are often late and have to be included in the next period's tabulation. Also, it is not entirely descriptive of the *total* attrition of the "Columbia" panel, as households may have continued to send in diaries even though they did not return the mail questionnaire or were missed by one or more telephone interviews. For the analysis in this report, where little reliance is placed on the results of the telephone interviews, the number of households returning diaries is quite appropriate (see Table C–1).

The actual performance of the "Columbia" panel can be seen from Table C–2, which compares the initial and continuing attrition, as a proportion of the initial panel size, to the average performance of eight panels, as reported in Bucklin and Carman.[1] The similarity of the performance of the "Columbia" panel to other published panels is encouraging. The initial dropout rate is lower in the "Columbia" panel primarily because of different recruitment procedures. There is a tendency in panel recruitment by personal interview for respondents to want to be agreeable, or perhaps to succumb to momentary pressure to participate. This increases the chance that second thoughts, after the departure of the interviewer, might lead to a decision to not participate, despite having agreed previously. The somewhat higher continuing attrition rate is a combination of vacationers deciding to dropout during the summer,

Table C–1—Attrition of "Columbia" and "Control" Panels Over a Five Month Period

(Both panels started with 1100 households.)

	NUMBER OF HOUSEHOLDS RETURNING DIARIES		Cumulative Difference Columbia Minus Control Panel
Period	Columbia Panel	Control Panel	
1	832a	808	+24
2	934	930	+28
3	891b	865	+54
4	859	915	−2
5	768c	786	−20
6	825	866	−61
7	701	770	−130
8	742	819	−207
9	718	770	−259
10	678	707	−288
Average difference over the ten periods			−28

a Influence of mail questionnaire felt here.
b Influence of first telephone interview felt here.
c Influence of second telephone interview felt here.

1. Two panels reported in Table 6–1 are not included in the average, because their performance was so abysmal.

and the effect of the unannounced extra work load of two telephone interviews during the first two and one half months. Had the "Columbia" panel been continued for another few months, without further interference, it is probable that the "continuing" attrition rate would have approached 3.0 to 3.5 per cent per month.

When the "Columbia" and "Control" panels are compared, it appears that the extra work load initially encouraged a high level of cooperation. Perhaps the mail questionnaire increased the level of interest, while the two telephone interviews served as reminders to return the purchase diary that was on hand. These positive effects were short lived indeed. In the three bi-weekly periods, following the second telephone interview "reminder," the cumulative difference in the return rates of the two panels was 65 per cent of the total cumulative difference in ten periods. It is difficult to say whether this is due to (1) the release of pressure on the panel members, (2) a manifestation of resentment at the unexpected work load, or (3) a reflection of some intrinsic difference in the two panels. The last hypothesis is being tested as part of the Research Project on Buyer Behavior.

SENSITIZATION TO PRODUCT CLASS AND "ANALYSIS" BRAND

The major problem in evaluating the effect of sensitization is that the product itself represents a highly "discretionary" purchase. It is a convenience food for which many alternatives exist. So it is hardly surprising that more households in the "Columbia" panel bought the product when they had been alerted to the researchers' interest in it. Although the effect is large in percentage terms, the actual number of households who became interested in the product because of the mail questionnaire and the single telephone interview is reasonably small. However, a disproportionately large percentage of the people who became interested in the product also bought the "analysis" brand because this was the brand toward which most of the questions were directed. As shown in Table C-3, the biasing effect was more pronounced on the brand's share of total buyers of the product than on the share of total

Table C-2—Initial and Continuing Attrition—Columbia Panel versus Average of Eight Other Panels[a]

(Percent of *initial* panel size; after refusals eliminated)

	Columbia Panel	Average of Eight Published Panels
Dropout during first 3 to 6 weeks	19.4%	20.2%
Continuing Attrition rate (Percent per month—using running average number of returns)	4.3	2.7

a Bucklin and Carman, 1967, page 14.

179

volume. The data in Table C–3 represent averages over the entire ten periods and conceal a great deal of period-by-period variation. Figure C–1 is a graph of the differences for each period.

Although these data on the influence of specific brand questions are hardly encouraging, they should not be construed as cause for alarm or loss of confidence in the results. First of all, if the "analysis" brand's *true* share of households buying the product was 40 per cent (which it was not) the share recorded by the "Columbia" panel would have been 45.7 per cent. This is the kind of difference that is often found when store audit share data are compared with panel share data. Secondly, the fact that there is less distortion in the volume share than in the share of households buying suggests that the problem lies with the light buyers of the product, that is, those who have had less experience with the product and/or less firmly developed purchasing habits. Yet in the analysis of the attitude—behavior relationship there was very little difference between light and heavy buyers *so far as the shape of the relationship is concerned.* This finding is consistent with the argument put forward in Appendix A that sensitization does not affect relationships.

The argument above should be modified slightly to take into account the elimination of some one-time buyers from the analysis. This was done primarily to reduce the impact of "running-in" effects on behavior. Apparently some panel members feel guilty if they cannot report a purchase in a product category in the first one to three periods. Accordingly it was decided to eliminate 48 households who reported only one purchase of the product in the first three periods, and none subsequently, on the grounds that they were just trying to "please" the person who had asked them to join the panel. When this was done the difference between the two panels in the average percentage of households buying the "analysis" brand dropped from 14.3 per cent to 12.3 per cent. Because the one-time buyers purchased such a small volume, their elimination had no effect on the difference in the share of total volume accounted for by the "analysis" brand.

Several other adjustments had to be made before the final figure of 238 buyers of the product was reached. These are summarized in Table C–4.

Table C–3—Sensitization Toward "Analysis" Brand Due to Membership in Columbia Panel

$$\left(\frac{Columbia\ panel - Control\ panel}{Control\ panel}\right) \times 100\%)$$

(A) Difference in percentage of households buying product $= +24.1\%$
(B) Difference in percentage of households buying "analysis" brand $= +14.3\%$
(C) Difference in share of total volume accounted for by "analysis" brand $= +10.2\%$

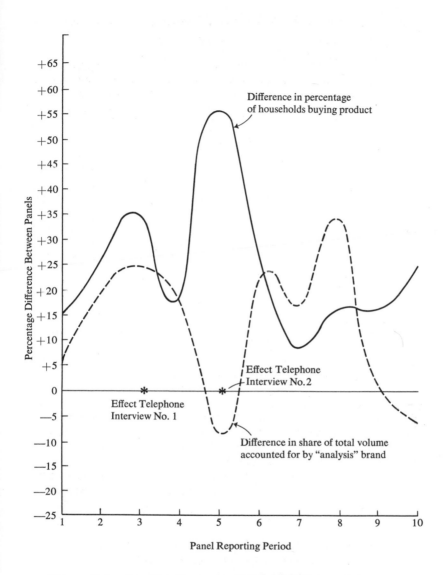

Figure C–1. **Sensitization toward "Analysis" brand due to membership in Columbia panel.**

Table C–4—Definition of Buyers of Product

Number of households reporting one or more purchases of the product = 336

Less: (1) Households making only one purchase in first three
periods   = 48
    (2) Panel dropouts (less than five periods of data available) = 35
    (3) Panel members who did not return mail questionnaires = 15   98

Number of households considered to be buyers   238

Less: Buyers without an initial attitude toward the analysis
Brand   = 18

     220

Appendix D

Characteristics of the Attitude Scales

A fundamental feature of the theoretical model developed in this report is the unidimensional scale of affect with equal-interval properties. Two different unidimensional scales were used in the process of testing the model, but they are assumed to be comparable in their ability to distribute respondents along a continuum. The purpose of this appendix is to describe some of the known characteristics of these two scales, with particular emphasis on the equal-interval assumption.

Thurstone Scales (Durables Panel)

Each appliance brand was rated on three trichotomous questions dealing respectively with willingness to recommend the brand to a friend, availability of maintenance, and level of product quality. The items within each of the three questions were non-cumulative, that is, acceptance of one item precluded acceptance of the other two. The problem was to assign some value to each of the three items accepted by the subject, so that a meaningful total score could be obtained by summing the three values. This meant that the individual item values had to be related to some common denominator, such as the degree of "favorableness," otherwise they could not be added together. Furthermore, the model required that similar differences between any two individual items, or total scores, measure the same psychological distance. In other words, equal-appearing intervals should represent equal psychological distances.

Thurstone's "Method of Equal-Appearing Intervals" (described in detail in Chapter 4 of Edwards, 1957) was adapted to the task of obtaining appropriate *scale values* for each item. First, 40 business school students and 30 housewives were asked to judge the degree of favorableness or unfavorableness of 30 statements about appliance brands. Among these statements were the nine that were actually used at the beginning of the durables panel. The instructions are shown in Figure D–1. It should be noted that only the middle and the extreme ends of the continuum were defined for the judges, in order that the intervals between successive categories would appear equal.

Figure D–I. Instructions to Judges of Attitude Statements

We would like you to judge the degree of favorableness, or unfavorableness, of a number of statements about appliance brands. These are general statements that could apply to any brand.

As you read each statement, imagine that someone you know has just made the statement to you, either in response to a question or as a general observation about the brand. We don't want you to agree or disagree with the statement, but just decide in your own mind how favorable or unfavorable it is.

There are eleven possible degrees of feeling that a statement might express, ranging from very unfavorable to neutral to very favorable. Please use the procedure outlined below to indicate your *judgment* of each statement:

1. Take the first eleven cards, which express the various degrees of feeling, and arrange them in front of you as follows:

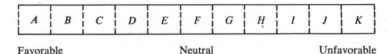

| A | B | C | D | E | F | G | H | I | J | K |

Favorable   Neutral   Unfavorable

2. Each statement is typed on a separate card. Think about each statement and decide which of the eleven categories of favorableness-unfavorableness is closest to the feeling expressed by that statement.

3. When you have decided, put the card with the statement on it in a pile below the card that indicates the degree of feeling.

4. After each statement has been assigned to a pile, review each pile to make sure that statements representing quite different feelings have not been put together.

5. Lastly, write the letter (A through K) that identifies the degree of favorableness or unfavorableness in the box below each statement.

Next, the frequency with which the nine statements were placed in each of the 11 categories of the continuum was determined. At this stage five judges were eliminated because they appeared to be responding in terms of their own agreement or disagreement with the statements. This can be attributed to carelessness in reading the instructions, as no actual brand names were used in any of the statements.

The actual scale value for each item was taken to be the median of the frequency distribution of judgments. At the same time the interquartile range (Q) of the judgments was used to provide a measure of the variation of the distribution of judgments. Large values of the interquartile range are usually a sign that the statement is ambiguous. In such cases the assumption that the item represents the same scale position for judges and subjects is invalid. Fortunately none of the nine items had a Q value greater than 2.0, and the majority were close to 1.5, indicating substantial agreement among the judges.

The *scoring procedure* for the responses to the attitude questions in the panel interview had to be modified somewhat from the usual Thurstone procedure of averaging the scale values of the items accepted. This became necessary when it was found that the three items within each question covered very different ranges of values. For example, in one question the values of the two extreme items were 2.0 and 5.8 (where the maximum possible range was 0 to 10), while in another question scale values ranged from 0.1 to 8.3. In order to make all three questions comparable it was decided to give the most favorable item a score of 0, and to add one-third the distance from the most favorable item to the item chosen to the total score. Thus, in the question on availability of maintenance, the most favorable response had a scale value of 1.8, while the most unfavorable response had a scale value of 8.4. If the respondent chose the latter item her total score was increased by:

$$\frac{8.4 - 1.8}{3} = 2.2$$

There are several other advantages to this incremental scoring system, in addition to compensating for the variable discriminatory power of the questions. One is that it permitted adjustment for the level of awareness. The assumption was that unaided recall, or "top of mind," awareness of a brand name implied a more intense attitude than if the brand name was merely "heard of." As we noted in Chapter 2 a more intense attitude is likely to be a better predictor, other things being equal. Unfortunately there is no evidence on the degree of effect of increased intensity. Accordingly it was decided to adjust the total score by the conservative value of $+1.0$ when the recall of the brand name was aided.

A further adjustment was made to take into account the pattern of responses. Here the assumption was made that several unfavorable responses

185

represented a more extreme position than the sum of the values of the seperate items. Also, none of the items provided an opportunity for the respondent to say, "this is the worst brand in the whole list," that is, a full range of responses was not possible. Again, a conservative approach was taken that if two or more of the most unfavorable items were selected by the respondent, the total score would be adjusted upwards by $+0.5$.

Thurstone scales are often treated as interval scales, as they are in this report. Nonetheless there is a significant body of findings which lead some researchers to conclude that the assumption about their interval nature is "dubious" (Selltiz et al., 1964, page 365). The questionable aspect is the assumption that differences in judged locations of a specific item are random, where in fact applications of Thurstone scaling to statements about prejudices have uncovered marked differences between the scale positions of "pro" and "anti" judges. No similar analysis of judges have been reported in studies of brand attitudes. However, Edwards (1957, page 109) suggests that when there is no ego-involvement, it is likely that scale values are independent of the attitudes of judges. In the analysis of appliance brand attitudes, in this report, there was really no opportunity for ego-involvement because the attitude statements to be judged were couched in very general terms. Also, we noted that there was a high degree of judgmental consensus on the meaning of the statements (expressed as the inter-quartile range of judgments). In view of these facts we have some assurance that the scale does have the requisite equal-interval property.

Thurstone scaling has not been widely used in marketing, primarily because of the considerable effort required to collect and analyze a large number of item judgments before scores can be assigned to respondents. A more popular approach (described below) is to give the respondent an equal-interval scale, from which the attitude scores can be obtained directly.

Semantic Differential Scales (Non-Durables Panel)

Recall from Chapter 4 that the measure of attitude, which was related to purchase behavior, was a single, seven-point, bi-polar, "general liking" semantic differential scale. Twelve other scales, dealing with specific attributes, were also used, but contributed very little to the prediction of behavior. Such reliance on one scale raises a number of questions: Is the semantic differential the best available brand rating scale for inclusion in a mail questionnaire? How well does it perform on the standard criteria for measuring instruments—particularly reliability and validity? And most important of all,

What evidence is there that the intervals between points are equal, as we have assumed in testing the attitude–behavior model?

One way to answer the first question, on the appropriateness of the semantic differential scale, is merely to note its widespread usage in a variety of marketing problems, for instance, in Barclay (1964), Landon (1962), Mindak (1961), and Mukherjee (1965), among others. More objective evidence comes from a large comparative study by Crespi (1964). He took three different rating scales: (1) A five-point Likert type scale with each position identified by a phrase, (2) a ten-point numerical scale, ranging from $+5$ to -5, with provision for recording "don't know" responses and, (3) a five-point Ladder scale with the bottom rung equal to 1, and the top rung equal to 5. Each of the three scale types were used to rate the performance of six industries, and were administered to a national probability sample of 500 persons. His conclusions suggest that a seven-point semantic differential scale is as good or better than any alternative. "In the U.S. at least, numerical rating scales are easier for most adults to use than are verbal rating scales. . . . Scales with an odd number of positions produce lower 'don't know' percentages than do those with an even number of positions. . . . The findings are somewhat inconclusive regarding the number of scale positions that should be used, though they suggest that about ten or eleven positions may be about the upper limit" (Crespi, 1964, page 516). Crespi also concluded that any numerical scale could be improved by the use of pictorial devices. Abrams (1966, page 191) has found that the sensitivity of numerical scales for rating brands can be improved by making the scale asymmetrical, and supplementing the numerical positions by comparisons with other products, such as, "below average, about average, a little better, a lot better, one of the best, or none better." No doubt the symmetrical scale used in this study could have been improved by these suggestions, but in general the basic scale design seems satisfactory.

The *reliability* (degree of reproducibility in over-time measures) of the semantic differential has been extensively studied by Osgood *et al.* (1957). They report that, "The average error of measurement . . . [is] always less than a single scale unit (approximately three-quarters of a scale unit) and for evaluative scales averages about half a scale unit. This means that we can expect subjects, on the average, to be accurate within a single unit of the scale, which for practical purposes is satisfactory (page 132). Actually, the absolute over-time deviation was zero in 54.0 per cent of the item responses, and one in 32.6 per cent of the responses. More recent work by Norman (1959), unfortunately using a very small sample, indicates that the semantic differential may be less reliable than Osgood *et al.* have claimed. He found an average shift of 1.07 units after four weeks. Of greater interest is the comparison Norman makes between the actual unit discrepancy (or shift) and the maximum unit discrepancy possible. The maximum depends on the initial position, that is, if the initial position were one, the greatest change would be six (a move to the other end of the scale) while if the initial position were two the greatest change would be five, and so forth. He found that the actual shift was 23.0 per cent of the maximum possible across all scales. Taking evaluative scales alone the actual shift was only 13.9 per cent of the maximum possible shift, (equal to an average shift of 0.65 units, a result very close to that reported by Osgood). The actual shift *seems* to decline as the concept becomes closer to the person's every-day experience, although Norman does not address this issue. Both sets of results are quite encouraging in view of the fact that we are using a purely evaluative scale.

The usual meaning of *validity*, where the instrument measures what it is supposed to measure, is not the primary concern here. Where this type of validity has been investigated (Osgood *et al.*, 1957, page 143; and Barclay, 1964, page 33) the results have been positive. Of greater significance is the validity of the equal interval assumption. Two methods of testing this assumption have been used, which are fully described in Osgood (1957, pages 146–153). The first method used Thurstone's method of equal appearing intervals to estimate the length of each interval for nine concepts. The deviations of these lengths from the lengths assumed by the semantic differential were found to well within the errors of measurement found in the reliability studies. Nonetheless there was a fairly consistent tendency for the lengths between extreme categories to be somewhat larger than between middle categories. The second method, of testing the equal-interval property, made use of the fact that the adverbial qualifiers "slightly, quite," and "extremely" are often used to describe the intensity of scale positions in respondent instructions. Separate analysis of these adverbs showed that adjacent qualifiers varied by "almost perfectly equal increasing degrees of intensity" (Osgood *et al.*, 1957, page 152). After reviewing these findings Osgood arrived ar the tentative conclusion, "that the scaling properties assumed with the semantic differential have some basis other than mere assumption."

Appendix E

Supporting Tables for
Chapter 5

This appendix includes:

(1) Basic *information* variables and associated factors for the durables panel,
(2) Construction of indices that are used as basic information variables,
(3) Basic *demographic* variables and associated factors for the durables panel,
(4) Univariate comparison of durables criterion groups on all explanatory variables,
(5) Factor analysis of classification variables for non-durables panel. These data have been incorporated to provide further insights into the structure of the variables used in this part of the study,
(6) Description of indices used to construct classification variables for non-durables data,
(7) Univariate comparison of non-durables criterion group on all explanatory variables.

Table E-1—Basic Information Variables and Associated Factors— Durables Panel

(Matrix of first four orthogonally rotated factors)

Description of Variable	Factor I	Factor II	Factor III	Factor IV
1. Number of times the household entertains in a month	—	—	—	0.670
2. Index of predisposition toward shopping (likelihood of taking time)	—	—	−0.789	—
3. Index of need for shopping oriented information	—	—	−0.401	0.718
4. Time spent reading magazines during the average weekday	0.848	—	—	—
5. Time spent reading newspapers	0.765	—	—	—
6. Time spent watching TV after 6 p.m.	—	−0.876	—	—
7. Number of magazines purchased	—	—	−0.567	—
8. Number of magazine subscriptions	0.430	0.539	—	0.461
Cumulative proportion of total variance	0.229	0.385	0.527	0.659

Notes: (1) All factors are estimated from the complete panel of 150 households.
(2) Loadings of less than 0.40 are not shown.
(3) Factor I = Exposure to print media.
Factor II = Choice of print media versus television.
Factor III = Desire for shopping oriented information.
Factor IV = (This last factor was ultimately not used, because it could not be related to a theoretical construct).

Figure E–2—Description of "Information" Indices

(A) Index of predisposition toward shopping (likelihood of taking time to shop)

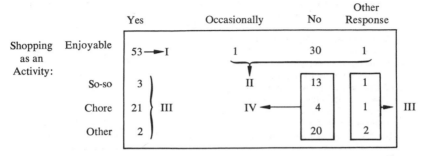

(B) Index of desire for shopping-oriented information (and assistance)

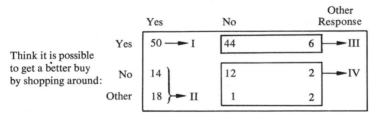

Note: Arrows indicate the index category.

Table E–2—Basic Demographic Variables and Associated Factors— Durables Panel

(Matrix of first four orthogonally rotated factors)

Description of Variable	Factor I	Factor II	Factor III	Factor IV
1. Urban, Surburban, Rural classification (high score = urban)	—	—	—	−0.964
2. Stage in life cycle (head of household)	—	0.769	—	—
3. Occupation of head of household	−0.553	—	—	—
4. Education of head of household	0.713	—	—	—
5. Number of years head has been married	—	0.844	—	—
6. Annual income before taxes	0.783	—	—	—
7. Discretionary income	0.745	—	—	—
8. Expected change in family income (in next 6 months) as a percentage of total income	—	—	−0.748	—
9. Amount of savings, investments, or reserve funds	—	—	0.596	—
Cumulative proportion of total variance	0.247	0.413	0.540	0.646

Notes: (1) All factors are estimated from the complete panel of 150 households.

(2) Loadings of less than 0.40 are not shown.

(3) Factor I = Socio-economic status (this factor was ultimately not used, because it could not be related to a theoretical construct).

Factor II = Married life cycle (of head of household).

Factor III = Anticipated economic constraints.

Factor IV = Access to stores (this factor is almost exclusively loaded on the rural, surburban, urban classification).

Table E–3—Univariate Comparison of Durables Criterion Groups on All Explantory Variables

	Criterion Group I (n = 30)	Criterion Group II (n = 19)
1. Number of products in inventory	5.50	5.53
2. Size of largest brand cluster	2.63	2.53
3. Married life cycle	−0.02	−0.01
4. Anticipated economic constraints	0.22	−0.24
5. Access to stores	−0.17	0.32
6. Exposure to print media	0.28	−0.13
7. Choice of print media versus TV	−0.11	−0.18
8. Desire for shopping oriented information	0.10	−0.27
9. Additions to inventory	3.10	2.74
10. Repair experience	1.33	1.58
11. Number of changes during the time of the panel	1.17	1.47
12. Number of brands aware of	3.03	2.68
13. Average attitude toward brands not purchased	1.94	2.44
14. Range of attitudes	3.79	2.87

Note: Variables 3 to 8 inclusive are standard normal deviates.

Table E-4—Factor Analysis of Classification Variables for the Non-Durables Panel

(Matrix of first six orthogonally rotated variables)

Description of Classification Variable	Factor I	Factor II	Factor III	Factor IV	Factor V	Factor VI
1. Self-perceived impulsiveness in food purchasing (index)	—	—	—	0.504	—	−0.435
2. Number of visitors at house in past seven days	—	—	—	—	0.698	—
3. Number of invitations to visit friends in past seven days	—	—	—	—	0.760	—
4. Weekday television viewing	—	0.578	—	—	—	—
5. Economy consciousness (index)	—	—	—	—	—	0.646
6. Interest in the differences among brands of products related to the one under study.	—	—	−0.874	—	—	—
7. Confidence in ability to judge between different brands of products related to the one under study.	—	—	−0.862	—	—	—
8. Self-perceived time pressure (index)	—	−0.553	—	0.493	—	—
9. Size of rural or urban area	—	—	—	0.727	—	—
10. Household size	0.938	—	—	—	—	—
11. Age of housewife	−0.601	—	—	—	—	—
12. Number and age of children in family (index)	0.907	—	—	—	—	—
13. Education of housewife	—	0.627	—	—	—	—
14. Occupation of head of household	—	—	—	—	—	−0.677
15. Number of hours housewife employed	—	0.660	—	—	—	—
16. Total household Income	—	—	—	—	—	0.610
Cumulative Proportion of Total Variance	0.170	0.294	0.400	0.478	0.552	0.624

Notes: (1) All factors are estimated from the 238 buyers of the product class under study.
(2) Loadings of less than 0.40 are not shown.
(3) Definition of factors:
Factor I = *Family life cycle* (high score = large family with a younger wife).
Factor II = *Leisure time availability and education* (high score = working housewife with a better than average education who feels rushed and has no time for television).
Factor III = *Concern over brand differences and confidence in brand judgments* (low score = low interest and confidence in brand judgments).
Factor IV = *Shopping pattern and life style* (high score = urban housewife, without too many demands on her time, who can afford to be impulsive).
Factor V = *Sociability* (high score = many visitors and invitations).
Factor VI = *Pressure for economy in buying* (high score = prosperous group without a great deal of concern for economy).

Table E–5—Description of Indices Used to Construct Classification Variables

(A) *Index of self-perceived impulsiveness* in food purchasing
   (+ = impulsive response, weighted 1, and − = other response, weighted 2)

—The question used to form this index was:

We would like to get your opinions on a few things that women's television programs and articles in women's magazines discuss a great deal. Would you say that the following statements are true for you?

	True	Not True
I quite often buy things on the spur of the moment.	(+)	(−)
I like to wait to hear how my friends like something before I try it myself.	(−)	(+)
When I'm in the grocery store, I am likely to reach out and pick up a new food just for the fun of it.	(+)	(−)
I don't like to buy anything the very first time I think of it.	(−)	(+)
I am the kind of woman who will try almost any new food once.	(+)	(−)

—The respondent's score on this index is the sum of the weighted responses to the five items above. Possible scores range from a minimum of five to a maximum of 10.

(B) *Index of economy consciousness*

—The items used to form this index were:

(a) The budget determines what we eat:
   All of the time (1) Most of the time (2) Sometimes (3) Never (4).
(b) I check the prices of the food items I buy:
   All of the time (1) Most of the time (2) Sometimes (3) Never (4).
(c) The difference in price between the various brands of packaged foods interests me:
   A great deal (1) Quite a lot (2) Only a little (3) Not at all (4).
(d) I go to stores, where I don't usually shop, in order to take advantage of food sales:
   Every chance I get (1) Almost every chance (2) Seldom (3) Never (4).

—The respondent's score on this index is the sum of the weighted responses to the four items above. Possible scores range from four, which is extremely economy conscious, to sixteen which is not at all concerned with economy.

(C) *Index of self-perceived time pressure*
                    (+ = presence of time pressure).

—The items used to form this index were:

	Yes	No
Do you often wish you had more to do?	(−)	(+)
Do you have so much else to do that you can't spend much time doing things around the house?	(+)	(−)
Do you sometimes feel that two people could not do all you have to do?	(+)	(−)
Does time sometimes hang heavy on your hands?	(−)	(+)

—The respondent's score on this index is the sum of the responses, when + responses are weighted one, and − responses are weighted two. Possible scores range from 4, which is extreme time pressure, to 8 which is none.

194

Table E–5   Continued

(D) *Index of presence of children by age groups* (weighted values)

0 = no children
1 = under 6 years only
3 = 6–12 years only
4 = 13–17 years only
5 = under 6 and 6–12 only
6 = under 6 and 13–17 only
7 = 6 to 12 and 13 to 17 only
9 = all three age groups

Table E–6—Univariate Comparisons of Non-Durables Criterion Groups on All Explanatory Variables

(Group Mean Values)

	CRITERION GROUPS				
	Group I	Group II	Group X	Group Y	Non-Buyers
Determinants of Stability					
1. Interest in brand differences	5.76	6.55	6.63	6.62	6.65
2. Confidence in judgments	5.69	6.41	7.37	6.57	6.51
Buying Style					
3. Impulsiveness	7.14	6.53	6.58	6.84	6.60
4. Economy consciousness	7.96	8.28	8.75	7.95	8.27
5. Time pressure	5.64	5.34	5.63	5.70	5.36
Demand, Store, Price response					
6. Units purchased	20.71	14.97	10.62	26.31	9.26
7. Average price paid	27.21	26.90	26.62	25.84	27.49
8. Range of prices paid	3.85	3.24	2.01	5.10	1.84
9. Dealing dummy variable	0.42	0.53	0.33	0.36	0.39
10. Store activity	0.53	0.60	0.45	0.47	0.29
Exposure to Information					
11. Number of visitors	5.39	5.95	5.26	5.25	5.04
12. Number of invitations	1.28	1.27	1.08	1.26	1.14
13. Television viewing (inverse of hours of viewing)	17.72	16.79	17.29	16.84	17.34
Socioeconomic, Demographic					
14. Size of city	4.40	5.32	5.20	4.52	5.27
15. Size of household	2.57	3.23	3.41	3.21	3.22
16. Age of housewife	48.25	44.65	47.00	47.60	43.70
17. Number of children	1.46	2.35	2.95	2.31	2.19
18. Education of housewife	12.36	13.07	12.26	12.54	12.70
19. Occupation	5.58	5.69	5.84	5.79	5.36
20. Household income	3.83	4.34	4.20	4.21	4.65
21. Hours employed	15.42	16.41	12.54	11.74	15.31

Bibliography

Abrams, Jack, "An Evaluation of Alternative Rating Devices for Consumer Research," *Journal of Marketing Research*, **3** (May 1966), 189–194.

Achenbaum, Alvin A., Address to 1966 Fall Conference, Advertising Research Foundation (October 1966b).

———, "An Answer to One of the Unanswered Questions About the Measurement of Advertising Effectiveness," in *Proceedings: Annual Conference, Advertising Research Foundation.* New York: October 1966c.

———, "Is Copy Testing a Predictive Tool?" *Proceedings Tenth ARF Annual Conference* (October 6, 1964).

———, "Knowledge Is a Thing Called Measurement," in Lee Adler and Irving Crespi (editors), *Attitude Research at Sea.* Chicago: American Marketing Association, 1966a.

———, "Relevant Measures of Consumer Attitude." Paper presented to the June 1967 Conference of the American Marketing Association, Toronto, Canada.

Adams, F. Gerard, "Consumer Attitudes, Buying Plans and Purchase of Durable Goods: A Principal Components Time Series Approach," *The Review of Economics and Statistics* (November 1964).

———, "Prediction with Consumer Attitudes: The Time Series–Cross Section Paradox," *The Review of Economics and Statistics*, (November 1965), 367–378.

Allison, Harry E., Charles J. Zwick, and Ayres Brunser, "Recruiting and Maintaining a Consumer Panel," *Journal of Marketing*, **22** (April 1958), 377–390.

Amstutz, Arnold E., "*Management Use of Computerized Micro-Analytic Behavioral Simulations,*" (unpublished working paper, MIT, March 1966).

Appel, Valentine F., "Attitude Change: Another Dubious Method for Measuring Advertising Effectiveness," in Lee Adler and Irving Crespi (editors), *Attitude Research at Sea.* Chicago: American Marketing Association, 1966.

Axelrod, Joel N., "Attitude Measures That Predict Purchase," *Journal of Advertising Research*, **8** (March 1968), 3–18.

Banks, Seymour, *Experimentation in Marketing.* New York: McGraw-Hill, 1965.

———, "The Measurement of the Effect of a New Packaging Material upon Preference and Sales," *The Journal of Business*, **23** (1950), 71–80.

———, "The Relationship Between Preference and Purchase of Brands," *The Journal of Marketing*, **15** (1950–51), 145–157.

———, "Some Correlates of Coffee and Cleanser Brand Shares," *Journal of Advertising Research*, (June 1961).

Barclay, William D., "The Semantic Differential as an Index of Brand Attitude, *Journal of Advertising Research*, **4** (March 1964), 30–33.

Bauer, Raymond A., "Consumer Behavior as Risk Taking," in Robert S. Hancock (editor), *43rd National Conference Proceedings*. Chicago: American Marketing Association, 1960.

———, "Attitudes, Verbal Behavior and Other Behavior," in Lee Adler and Irving Crespi (editors), *Attitude Research at Sea*. Chicago: American Marketing Association, 1966.

Beldo, Leslie A., "Introduction to Attitude Research and Management Decisions," in George L. Baker (editor), *Effective Marketing Coordination*. Chicago: American Marketing Association, 1961.

Berelson, Bernard L., Paul F. Lazarsfeld, and William McPhee, *Voting*. Chicago: University of Chicago Press, 1954.

———, and Gary A. Steiner, *Human Behavior: An Inventory of Scientific Findings*. New York: Harcourt, Brace and World, 1964.

Berg, Thomas L., and Abe Shuchman, *Product Strategy and Management*. New York: Holt, Rinehart and Winston, 1963.

Berlyne, D. E. "Exploratory and Epistemic Behavior," in Sigmund Koch (editor), *Psychology: The Study of a Science*. New York: McGraw-Hill, 1963.

Bieri, James, "Attitudes and Arousal: Affect and Cognition in Personality Functioning," in Carolyn and Muzafer Sherif, (editors), *Attitude, Ego-Involvement and Change*. New York: John Wiley, 1967.

Binder, A., "Statistical Theory," in P. R. Farnsworth, O. McNemar, and Q. McNemar (editors), *Annual Review of Psychology*, **15** (1964), 277–310.

Blalock, Hubert M., and Ann B. Blalock, *Methodology in Social Research*. New York: McGraw-Hill, 1968.

Blankenship, A. B., "Let's Bury Paired Comparisons," *Journal of Advertising Research*, **6** (March 1966), 13–17.

Bogart, Leo, *Strategy in Advertising*. New York: Harcourt, Brace and World, 1967.

Boyd, Harper W., and Ralph L. Westfall, *An Evaluation of Continuous Consumer Panels as a Source of Marketing Information*. Chicago: American Marketing Association, 1960.

Brown, George H., "Measuring Consumer Attitudes Toward Products," *Journal of Marketing*, **14** (October 1950).

———, "The Automobile Buying Decision Within the Family," in Nelson N. Foote (editor), *Household Decision-Making*. New York: NYU Press, 1961, 193–199.

Bucklin, Louis P., and James M. Carman, *The Design of Research Panels: Conception and Administration of the Berkeley Food Panel*. Berkeley: Institute of Business and Economic Research, 1967.

Burdick, Eugene, and Arthur J. Brodbeck (editors), *American Voting Behavior*. New York: Free Press, 1959.

Burns, Arthur F., *The Frontiers of Economic Research*. Princeton: Princeton University Press, 1954.

Bush, R. R., and F. Mosteller, "Selected Quantitative Techniques," in Gardner Lindzey (editor), *Handbook of Social Psychology*. Cambridge, Mass.: Addison-Wesley, 1954.

———, and ———, *Stochastic Models for Learning*. New York: John Wiley, 1955.

Campbell, Angus, Philip E. Converse, Warren E. Miller, and Donald E. Stokes, *The American Voter*. New York: John Wiley, 1960.

Campbell, D. T., "Social Attitudes and Other Acquired Behavioral Dispositions," in S. Koch (editor), *Psychology: A Study of a Science*. New York: McGraw-Hill, 1963.

———, and Keith N. Clayton, "Avoiding Regression Effects in Panel Studies of Communication Impact," *Studies in Public Communication*, **3** (1961), 99–118.

Caplovitz, David, *The Poor Pay More*. New York: Free Press, 1963.

Carey, James W., "Personality Correlates of Persuasibility," in Stephen A. Greyser (editor), *Toward Scientific Marketing*. Chicago: American Marketing Association, 1963, 30–43.

Carman, James M., "Brand Attitudes and Linear Learning Models," *Journal of Advertising Research*, **6** (June 1966), 23–31.

———, and John L. Stromberg, "A Comparison of Some Measures of Brand Loyalty." Unpublished working paper, Institute of Business and Economic Research, University of California, Berkeley, July 1967.

Carroll, John B., "The Nature of Data; or How to Choose a Correlation Coefficient," *Psychometrika*, **26** (1961), 347–361.

Clover, Vernon T., "Measuring Firmness with which Opinions Are Held," *Public Opinion Quarterly*, **14** (Summer, 1950), 338–340.

Cohen, Arthur R., *Attitude Change and Social Influence*. New York: Basic Books, 1964.

Coleman, James S., *Introduction to Mathematical Sociology*. New York: Free Press, 1964.

Colley, Russell, H., (editor), *Defining Advertising Goals for Measured Advertising Results*. New York: Association of National Advertisers, 1961.

Cooley, W. W., and P. R. Lohnes, *Multivariate Procedures for the Behavioral Sciences*. New York: John Willey, 1962.

Couch, Arthur, and Kenneth Keniston, "Yeasayers and Naysayers: Agreement Response Set as a Personality Variable," *Journal of Abnormal and Social Psychology*, **60** (March 1960), 151–174.

Coulson, John S., "Buying Decisions Within the Family and the Consumer-Brand Relationship," in Joseph W. Newman (editor), *On Knowing the Consumer*. New York: John Wiley, 1966a, 59–66.

———, "The Influence of Believabilty and Amount of Advertising," in Newman, *op. cit.* (1966b), 116–124.

Cox, Donald F., and Raymond A. Bauer, "Self-Confidence and Persuasibility in Women," *Public Opinion Quarterly*, **28** (Fall 1964), 453–466.

Crespi, Irving, "A Comparison of Three Rating Scales," in Robert M. Kaplan (editor), *The Marketing Concept in Action*. Chicago: American Marketing Association, 1964, 508–517.

———, *Attitude Research*. Chicago: American Marketing Association, 1965.

Cunningham, Ross M., "Brand Loyalty—What, Where, How Much?" *Harvard Business Review*, **34** (January–February 1956), 116–128.

Day, George S., "Some Problems in the Sequential Application of Multivariate Techniques," in *Proceedings, American Marketing Association*. Chicago: American Marketing Association, 1968.

Day, George S., "Mathematical Models of Attitude Change for Evaluating New Product Introductions." Unpublished working paper, Stanford University, Graduate School of Business, 1969.

———, and Henry Assael, "Attitudes and Awareness as Predictors of Market Share," *Journal of Advertising Research*, 8 (December 1968), 3–10.

DeFleur, M. L., and F. R. Westie, "Verbal Attitudes and Overt Acts: An Experiment on the Salience of Attitudes," *American Sociological Review*, 23 (1958), 667–673.

———, and ———, "Attitude as a Scientific Concept," *Social Forces*, 42 (1963) 17–31.

Dixon, W. J. (editor), *Biomedical Computer Programs*. Los Angeles: University of California, 1964.

Dollard, John, "Under What Conditions Do Opinions Predict Behavior?" *Public Opinion Quarterly* (Winter 1948–49), 623–632.

Doob, Leonard W., "The Behavior of Attitudes," *Psychological Review*, 54 (1947), 135–156.

Dubois, Cornelius, "The Story of Brand XL: How Consumer Attitudes Affected Its Market Position," *Public Opinion Quarterly*, 24 (Fall 1960), 479–480.

Duesenberry, J. S., *Income, Saving and the Theory of Consumer Behavior*. Cambridge: Harvard University Press, 1952.

Eagly, Alice H., "Involvement as a Determinant of Response to Favorable and Unfavorable Information," *Journal of Personality and Social Psychology Monograph*, 7 (November 1967), Whole Number 643.

Edwards, Allen L., *Techniques of Attitude Scale Construction*. New York: Appleton-Century-Crofts, 1957.

Ehrenberg, A. S. C., "A Study of Some Potential Biases in the Operation of a Consumer Panel," *Applied Statistics*, 9 (March 1960), 20–27.

———, "Estimating the Proportion of Loyal Buyers," *Journal of Marketing Research*, 1 (February 1964), 56–59.

———, "Laws in Marketing: A Tail Piece," *Applied Statistics*, 15 (November 1966), 257–267.

Ehrlich, D., *et al.*, "Post Decision Exposure to Relevant Information," *Journal of Abnormal and Social Psychology*, 57 (January 1957), 98.

Ellul, Jacques, *Propaganda: The Formation of Men's Attitudes*. New Tork: Alfred A. Knopf, 1965.

Engel, James F., David T. Kollatt, and Roger D. Blackwell, *Consumer Behavior*. New York: Holt, Rinehart and Winston, 1968.

Evans, Franklin B., "Selling as a Dyadic Relationship—A New Approach," *American Behavioral Scientist* 6 (May 1963) 76–79.

Farley, John U., "Brand Loyalty and the Economics of Information," *Journal of Business* (1964b) 370–379.

———, "Why Does Brand Loyalty Vary Over Products?" *Journal of Marketing Research*, 1 (November 1964a) 9–14.

———, and Alfred A. Kuehn, "Stochastic Models of Brand Switching," in George Schwartz, (editor), *Science in Marketing*, New York: John Wiley, 1965, 446–464.

Feldman, Shel, "Motivational Aspects of Attitudinal Elements," in S. Feldman (editor), *Cognitive Consistency*. New York: Academic Press, 1966, 75–108.

Feldt, Leonard S., "The Use of Extreme Groups to Test for the Presence of a Relationship," *Psychometrika*, **26** (September 1961), 307–315.

Fendrich, James M., "A Study of the Association Among Verbal Attitudes, Commitment and Overt Behavior in Different Experimental Situations," *Social Forces* (1965).

Festinger, Leon, *A Theory of Cognitive Dissonance*. Evanston: Row, Peterson, 1957.

——, "Behavioral Support for Opinion Change," *Public Opinion Quarterly*, **29** (Fall 1964), 405–417.

Fishbein, Martin, "An Investigation of the Relationships Between Beliefs About an Object and the Attitude Toward That Object," *Human Relations*, **16** (1963), 233–239.

——, "The Relationship Between Beliefs, Attitudes and Behavior" (unpublished paper, 1965).

Frank, Ronald E., "Use of Transforms," *Journal of Marketing Research*, **3** (August 1966), 247–254.

——, "Is Brand Loyalty a Useful Basis for Market Segmentation?" *Journal of Advertising Research*, **7** (June 1967), 27–33.

——, W. F. Massy, and D. G. Morrison, "Bias in Multiple Discriminant Analysis," *Journal of Marketing Research* **2** (August 1965), 250–258.

——, ——, and ——, "The Determinants of Innovative Behavior with Respect to a Branded, Frequently Purchased Food Product," in L. George Smith (editor), *Reflections on Progress in Marketing*, Chicago: American Marketing Association, 1964, 312–323.

Freedman, J. L., "Involvement, Discrepancy and Change," *Journal of Abnormal and Social Psychology*, **69** (1964), 290–295.

Gage, N. L., and B. B. Chatterjee, "The Psychological Meaning of Acquiescence Set: Further Evidence," *Journal of Abnormal and Social Psychology*, **60** (1960), 280–283.

Ghiselli, Edwin E., "Moderating Effects and Differential Reliability and Validity," *Journal of Applied Psychology*, **47** (April 1963), 81–86.

Glock, Charles Y., and Francesco M. Nicosia, "Sociology and the Study of Consumers," *Journal of Advertising Research*, **3** (September 1963), 21–27.

Goldberg, Samuel, *Introduction to Difference Equations*. New York: John Wiley, 1958.

Grandbois, Donald H., "The Role of Communication in the Family Decision-Making Process," in Stephen A. Greyser (editor), *Toward Scientific Marketing*. Chicago: American Marketing Association, 1963, 44–57.

——, and James F. Engel, "The Longitudinal Approach to Studying Marketing Behavior," in Peter D. Bennett (editor), *Marketing and Economic Development*. Chicago: American Marketing Association, 1965, 502–221.

Green, Bert F., "Attitude Measurement," in Gardner Lindzey (editor), *Handbook of Social Psychology*. Cambridge, Mass.: Addison-Wesley, 1954.

Greenberg, Allan, "Paired Comparisons vs. Monadic Tests," *Journal of Advertising Research*, **3** (December 1963), 44–47.

Guilford, J. P., "When Not to Factor Analyze," *Psychological Bulletin*, **49** (1952).

Guttman, Louis, "The Principal Components of Scalable Attitudes," in Paul F.

Lazarsfeld (editor), *Mathematical Thinking in the Social Sciences*. New York: Free Press, 1954.

———, and Edward A. Suchman, "Intensity and a Zero Point for Attitude Analysis," *American Sociological Review*, **12** (1947), 55–67.

Harris, Douglas, "Predicting Consumer Reaction to Product Designs," *Journal of Advertising Research*, **4** (June 1964).

Haskins, Jack B., "Factual Recall as a Measure of Advertising Effectiveness," *Journal of Advertising Research*, **4** (March 1964), 2–8.

Himmelstrand, Ulf, "Verbal Attitudes and Behavior: A Paradigm for the Study of Message Transmission and Transformation," *Public Opinion Quarterly*, **24** (Summer 1960).

Hoel, P. G., *Introduction to Mathematical Statistics* (Third Edition). New York: John Wiley, 1954.

Hovland, C. I., I. L. Janis, and H. H. Kelley, *Communication and Persuasion*. New Haven: Yale University Press, 1953.

Howard, John A., *Marketing Management: Analysis and Planning*. Homewood, Ill.: Richard D. Irwin, 1963.

———, *Summary of The Theory of Buyer Behavior*, delivered to the Symposium on Consumer Behavior, The University of Texas, Austin, Texas, April 18, 1966.

———, and Jagdish N. Sheth, *The Theory of Buyer Behavior* (unpublished manuscript, 1966 and 1967).

Hyman, Herbert H., "Inconsistencies as a Problem of Attitude Research," *Journal of Social Issues*, **5** (1959), 38–42.

Ito, Rikuma, "Differential Attitudes of New Car Buyers," *Journal of Advertising Research*, **7** (March 1967), 38–42.

Janis, I., and S. Fesbach, "Effects of Fear-Arousing Communications," *Journal of Abnormal and Social Psychology*, **48** (1953), 78–92.

Juster, F. Thomas, *Anticipations and Purchases: An Analysis of Consumer Behavior*. Princeton: Princeton University Press, 1964.

———, "Consumer Buying Intentions and Purchase Probability," *Journal of the American Statistical Association*, **61** (September 1966).

Katona, George, "Attitude Change: Instability of Response and Acquisition of Experience, *Psychological Monographs*," **72**: 10 (1958), 1–38.

———, *Psychological Analysis of Consumer Behavior*. New York: McGraw-Hill, 1951.

———, *The Powerful Consumer*. New York: McGraw-Hill, 1960.

———, and Eva Mueller, "A Study of Purchase Decisions," in Lincoln Clark (editor), *Consumer Behavior: The Dynamics of Consumer Reaction*. New York: New York University Press, 1955, 30–87.

Katz, D., "The Functional Approach to the Study of Attitudes," *Public Opinion Quarterly*, **24** (Summer 1960).

———, and E. Stotland, "A Preliminary Statement to a Theory of Attitude Structure and Change," in S. Koch (editor), *Psychology: A Study of a Science*. New York: McGraw-Hill, 1959.

Katz, Elihu, and Paul Lazarsfeld, *Personal Influence*. New York: Free Press, 1955.

Kendall, Patricia, *Conflict and Mood: Factors Affecting Stability of Response*. New York: Free Press, 1954.

Kendall, Patricia L., and Katherine M. Wolf, "The Two Purposes of Deviant Case Analysis," in Paul F. Lazarsfeld and Morris Rosenberg, (editors), *The Language of Social Research.* New York: Free Press, 1955, 167–169.

Kenkel, William F., "Decision-Making and the Life Cycle: Husband-Wife Interaction in Decision-Making and Decision Choices," *The Journal of Social Psychology,* **54** (August 1961), 255–262.

Keynes, John Maynard, *The General Theory of Employment, Interest and Money.* New York: Harcourt, Brace, 1964

King, William R., "On Methods: Structural Analysis and Descriptive Functions," *Journal of Advertising Research,* **7** (June 1967), 39–43.

Kirsch, Arthur D., Philip K. Berger, and R. J. Belford, "Are Reports of Brands Bought Last Reliable and Valid?" *Journal of Advertising Research,* (June 1962).

Kosobud, Richard F., and James N. Morgan (editors), *Consumer Behavior of Individual Families Over Two and Three Years.* Ann Arbor: University of Michigan Press, 1964.

Kretch, D., and R. Crutchfield, *Theory and Problems of Social Psychology.* New York: McGraw-Hill, 1948.

Krugman, Herbert E., "The Impact of Television Advertising: Learning Without Involvement," *Public Opinion Quarterly,* **29** (1965), 349–356.

———, "The Measurement of Advertising Involvement," **30** (1966–67), 583–596.

Kuehn, A. A., "Consumer Brand Choice—A Learning Process?" in R. E. Frank, A. A. Kuehn, and W. F. Massy (editors), *Quantitative Techniques in Marketing Analysis.* Homewood: Richard D. Irwin, 1962, 390–403.

Landon, James A., "Attitudes Toward Commercial and Educational Television," *Journal of Advertising Research,* **2** (September 1962), 33–36.

Lane, Robert E., and David O. Sears, *Public Opinion.* Englewood Cliffs: Prentice-Hall, 1964.

Lang, Kurt, and Gladys Lang, "Ballots and Broadcasts: The Impact of Expectations and Election Day Perceptions on Voting Behavior." Presented to 1965 American Association of Public Opinion Research Conference.

Lavidge, Robert C., and Gary A. Steiner, "A Model for Predictive Measurements of Advertising Effectiveness," *Journal of Marketing,* **25** (October 1961), 59–62.

Lawley, D. N., and A. E. Maxwell, *Factor Analysis as a Statistical Method.* London: Butterworths, 1963.

Lazarsfeld, Paul F., "Sociological Reflections on Business: Consumers and Managers," in Robert A. Dahl, Mason Haire, and Paul F. Lazarsfeld, *Social Science Research on Business: Product and Potential.* New York: Columbia University Press, 1959, 99–156.

———, "The Use of Panels in Social Research," in B. Berelson and M. Janowitz (editors), *Reader in Public Opinion and Communications.* New York: Free Press, 1953, 511–519.

———, and Allen H. Barton, "Qualitative Measurement in the Social Sciences: Classification, Typologies and Indices," in Daniel Lerner and Harold D. Lasswell, (editors), *The Policy Sciences.* Stanford: Stanford University Press, 1951, 155–192.

———, Bernard Berelson, and Hazel Gaudet, *The Peoples Choice.* New York: Columbia University Press, 1944.

Lipset, Seymour M., Paul F. Lazarsfeld, Allen H. Barton, and Juan Linz, "The

Psychology of Voting: An Analysis of Political Behavior," in Gardner Lindzey, (editor), *Handbook of Social Psychology II*, Cambridge: Addison-Wesley, 1954, 1124–1175.

Lipstein, Benjamin, "A Mathematical Model of Consumer Behavior," *Journal of Marketing Research*, **2** (August 1965), 259–265.

Lunn, J. A., "Psychological Classification," *Commentary*, **8** (July 1966), 161–173.

McCroskey, *et al.*, "Attitude Intensity and the Neutral Point on Semantic Differential Scales," *Public Opinion Quarterly*, **30** (Winter 1967–68), 642–645.

Maloney, John C., "Attitude Measurement and Formation." Paper presented at the Test Market Design and Measurement Workshop, American Marketing Association, Chicago, April 21, 1966.

——, "Copy Testing: What Course Is It Taking?" *Proceedings, Ninth Annual Conference*. New York: Advertising Research Foundation, 1963, 89–94.

Massy, William F., *Costs of Uncertainty in Advertising Media Selection* (unpublished working paper, Carnegie Institute of Technology, December 1966).

——, "On Methods: Discriminant Analysis of Audience Characteristics," *Journal of Advertising Research*, **5** (March 1965), 39–48.

——, "Statistical Analysis of Relations Between Variables," in R. E. Frank, A. A. Kuehn, and W. F. Massy (editors), *Quantitative Techniques in Marketing Analysis*. Homewood, Ill.: Richard D. Irwin, 1962, 56–105.

Maxwell A. E. *Analyzing Qualitative Data*. New York: John Wiley, 1961.

Mendelsohn, Harold, "Ballots and Broadcasts: Exposure to Election Broadcasts and Terminal Voting Decisions." Presented to American Association of Public Opinion Research Conference.

Miller, David W., and Martin K. Starr, *Executive Decisions and Operations Research*. Englewood Cliffs: Prentice-Hall, 1960.

Miller, James, G., "Living Systems: Basic Concepts," *Behavioral Science*, **10** (July 1965), 193–237.

Mindak, William A., "Fitting the Semantic Differential to the Marketing Problem," *Journal of Marketing*, **25** (April 1961), 28–33.

Morgan, James N., and John A. Sonquist, "Problems in the Analysis of Survey Data, and a Proposal," *Journal of the American Statistical Association*, **58** (June 1963), 415–435.

Morris, Calvin, "Buying Games," in Dan Ailloni-Charas (editor), *Proceedings: National Conference on Research Design*. New York: American Marketing Association, 1964, 35–40.

Morrisett, Irving, "Consumer Attitudes, Expectations and Plans," in Likert and Hayes, (editor), *Some Applications of Behavioral Research*. Paris: UNESCO, 1955.

Morrison, D. G., R. E. Frank, and W. F. Massy, "A Note on Panel Bias," *Journal of Marketing Research*, **3** (February 1966), 85–88.

Moscovici, Serge, "Attitudes and Opinions," in *Annual Review of Psychology*, **14** (1963).

Moulson, T. J., "Danger Signals: How to Spot Erosion in Brand Loyalty," *Printers' Ink* (March 12, 1965), 55–61.

204

Mueller, Eva, "A Study of Purchase Decisions (Part 2)," in Lincoln H. Clark (editor), *Consumer Behavior*. New York: NYU Press, 1955, 33–87.

———, "Ten Years of Consumer Attitude Surveys: Their Forecasting Record," *Journal of American Statistical Association* (December 1963), 899 *et seq.*

Mukherjee, B. N., "A Factor Analysis of Some Qualitative Attributes of Coffee," *Journal of Advertising Research*, **5** (March 1965), 35–38.

Myers, James H., and William H. Reynolds, *Consumer Behavior and Marketing Management*. New York: Houghton Mifflin, 1967.

Myers, John G., "Determinants of Private Brand Attitudes," *Journal of Marketing Research*, **4** (February 1967), 73–81.

National Broadcasting Company *Strangers into Customers*. New York: NBC, 1955.

Newman, Joseph W. (editor), *On Knowing the Consumer*. New York: Wiley, 1966.

Nicosia, Francesco M., *Consumer Decision Processes: Marketing and Advertising Implications*. Englewood Cliffs: Prentice-Hall, 1966.

———, "Panel Designs and Analyses in Marketing," in Peter D. Bennett, (editor), *Marketing and Economic Development*. Chicago: American Marketing Association, 1965, 222–243.

Ortengren, John, "When Don't Research Panels Wear Out?" *Journal of Marketing*, **21** (April 1957), 442.

Osgood, C. E., G. J. Suci, and P. H. Tannenbaum, *The Measurement of Meaning*. Urbana: University of Illinois Press, 1957.

Oxenfeldt, Alfred R. *et al.*, *Insights into Pricing*. Belmont, California: Wadsworth, 1961.

Palda, Kristian S., "The Evaluation of Regression Results," in Stephen A. Greyser (editor), *Toward Scientific Marketing*. Chicago: American Marketing Association, 1963, 279–290.

———, "The Hypothesis of a Hierarchy of Effects: A Partial Evaluation," *Journal of Marketing Research*, **3** (February 1966), 13–26.

———, *The Measurement of Cumulative Advertising Effects*. Englewood Cliffs: Prentice-Hall, 1964.

Parfitt, John H., "A Comparison of Purchase Recall with Diary Panel Records," *Journal of Advertising Research*, **7** (September 1967), 16–31.

Peak, Helen, "Attitude and Motivation," in Marshall R. Jones (editor), *Nebraska Symposium on Motivation*. Lincoln: University of Nebraska Press, 1955, 149–188.

Peckham, James D., "The Consumer Speaks," *Journal of Marketing*, **27** (October 1963), 21–26.

Pessemier, Edgar A., and Douglas J. Tigert, "Personality, Activity, and Attitude Predictors of Consumer Behavior," in John S. Wright and Jac L. Goldstucker (editors), *New Ideas for Successful Marketing*. Chicago: American Marketing Association, 1966, 332–347.

———, Philip C. Burger, and ———, "Can New Product Buyers Be Identified?" *Journal of Marketing Research*, **4** (November 1967), 349–355.

Pratt, Robert W., Jr., "Consumer Behavior: Some Psychological Aspects," in George Schwartz (editor), *Science in Marketing*. New York: John Wiley, 1965, 98–136.

Pratt, Robert W., Jr., "Understanding the Decision Process for Consumer Goods: An Example of the Application of Longitudinal Analysis," in Peter D. Bennett (editor), *Marketing and Economic Development*. Chicago: American Marketing Association, 1965.

Ramond, Charles K., "Must Advertising Communicate to Sell?" *Harvard Business Review*, 43 (September–October 1965), 148–161.

Ray, Michael L., "Neglected Problems (Opportunities) in Attitude Research: Cross-Sectional, Longitudinal, Multiple and Unobtrusive Measurement." Paper presented to the American Marketing Association, August 1968 meeting.

Richmond, Samuel A., *Statistical Analysis*. New York: The Ronald Press, 1964.

Rogers, Everett M., *Diffusion of Innovations*. New York: Free Press, 1962.

———, and J. David Stanfield, *Adoption and Diffusion of New Products: Emerging Generalizations and Hypotheses* (unpublished paper presented at the Conference on the Application of Sciences to Marketing Management, Purdue University, July 12–15, 1966).

Rohloff, Albert C., "New Ways to Analyze Brand-to-Brand Competition," in Stephen A. Greyser (editor), *Toward Scientific Marketing*. Chicago: American Marketing Association, 1963, 224–232.

Rokeach, Milton, "Attitude Change and Behavior Change," *Public Opinion Quarterly*, 30 (Winter 1966–67), 529–550.

Roper, Burns W., "The Importance of Attitudes, the Difficulty of Measurement," John S. Wright and Jac L. Goldstucker (editors), *New Ideas for Successful Marketing*. Chicago: American Marketing Association, 1966.

———, "Some Unorthodox Solutions to Orthodox Problems," in Robert M. Kaplan (editor), *The Marketing Concept in Action*. Chicago: American Marketing Association, 1964, 519–530.

Rosenberg, Milton J., "An Analysis of Affective-Cognitive Inconsistency," in Rosenberg, *et al.* (editors), *Attitude Organization and Change*. New Haven: Yale University Press, 1960.

Rothman, James, "Formulation of an Index of Propensity to Buy," *Journal of Marketing Research*, 1 (May 1964), 21–25.

Ruch, Dudley M., "Limitations of Current Approaches to Understanding Brand Buying Behavior," in Joseph W. Newman (editor), *On Knowing the Consumer*. New York: John Wiley, 1966.

Saunders, David R., "Moderator Variables in Prediction," *Educational and Psychological Measurement*, 16 (1956,) 209–222.

Scott, W. A., "Attitude Measurement", G. Lindzey and E. Aronson, *Handbook of Social Psychology*. Cambridge: Addison-Wesley, 1968.

Selltiz, Claire, Marie Jahoda, Morton Deutsch, and Stuart W. Cook, *Research Methods in Social Relations*. New York: Holt, Rinehart and Winston, 1964.

Shaffer, James D., "The Reporting Period for a Consumer Purchase Panel," *Journal of Marketing*, 19 (January 1955), 252–257.

Sherif, Carolyn W., Muzafer Sherif, and Roger E. Nebergall, *Attitude and Attitude Change: The Social Judgment–Involvement Approach*. Philadelphia: Saunders, 1965.

Smith, Gail, "How GM Measures Ad Effectiveness," *Printers' Ink* (May 14, 1965).

Smith, M. Brewster, Jerome S. Bruner, and Robert W. White, *Opinions and Personality*. New York: John Wiley, 1956.

Smith, Wendall R., "Product Differentiation and Market Segmentation as Alternative Marketing Strategies," *Journal of Marketing*, **20** (July 1956), 3–8.

Sobel, Marion Gross, "Panel Mortality and Panel Bias," *Journal of the American Statistical Association*, **54** (March 1959), 52–68.

Sonquist, John A., and James N. Morgan, *The Detection of Interaction Effects: A Report on a Computer Program for the Selection of Optimal Combinations of Explanatory Variables*. Ann Arbor: Survey Research Center, University of Michigan, 1964, Monograph No. 35.

Stanton, Frank, "What Is Wrong with Test Marketing?" *Journal of Marketing*, **31** (April 1967), 43–48.

Stefflre, Volney, "Market Structure Studies" (unpublished manuscript, July 1965).

Steiner, Gary A., "Consumer Behavior: Where Do We Stand?" in Joseph W. Newman (editor), *On Knowing the Consumer*, New York: John Wiley, 1966, 205–212.

Stigler, George J., "The Economics of Information," *Journal of Political Economy* (June 1961), 213–25.

Stock, J. Stevens, Appendix to *A Study of the Magazine Market*. New York: Magazine Advertising Bureau of Magazine Publishers Association, 1960.

Stokes, Donald E., Angus Campbell, and Warren E. Miller, "Components of Electoral Decision," *American Political Science Review* (June 1958), 367–387.

Suchman, Edward A., "The Intensity Component in Attitude and Opinion Research," in S. A. Stouffer *et al.* (editors), *Measurement and Prediction*. New York: John Wiley, 1966.

Sudman, Seymour, "On the Accuracy of Recording of Consumer Panels, I and II," *Journal of Marketing Research*, **1** (May 1964a and August 1964b).

Suits, Daniel, "The Use of Dummy Variables in Regression Equations," *Journal of the American Statistical Association*, **52** (December 1957), 548–551.

Thurstone, L. L., "The Prediction of Choice," *Psychometrika*, **10** (December 1945), 237–253.

Tobin, James, "On the Predictive Value of Consumer Intentions and Attitudes," *Review of Economics and Statistics* (February 1959).

Tull, D. S., R. A. Boring, and M. H. Gonsior, "A Note on the Relationship of Price and Imputed Quality," *Journal of Business* (April 1964), 186–191.

Twedt, Dik Warren (editor), *A Survey of Marketing Research*. Chicago: American Marketing Association, 1963.

——, "How Important to Marketing Strategy Is the Heavy User?" *Journal of Marketing*, **28** (January 1964), 71–72.

United States Department of Agriculture, "Consumers' Preferences Among Bakers' White Breads of Different Formulas," *Marketing Research Report* No. 118 (Washington, D.C.: May 1956).

Vroom, Victor H., "Employee Attitudes," in George Fisk (editor), *The Frontiers of Management Psychology*. New York: Harper & Row, 1964, 127–143.

Webb, E. J., D. T. Campbell, R. D. Schwartz, and L. Sechrest, *Unobtrusive Measures: Nonreactive Research in the Social Sciences*. Chicago: Rand McNally, 1966.

Webster, Frederick E., Jr., "The 'Deal-Prone' Consumer," *Journal of Marketing Research*, **2** (May 1965), 186–189.

Weksel, W., and J. D. Hennes, "Attitude Intensity and the Semantic Differential," *Journal of Personality and Social Psychology*, **2** (1965), 91–94.

207

Wells, William D., "Computer Simulation of Consumer Behavior," *Harvard Business Review*, **41** (May–June 1963), 93–98.

———, "Measuring Readiness to Buy," *Harvard Business Review*, **39** (July–August 1961), 81–87.

———, "The Influences of Yeasaying Response Style," *Journal of Advertising Research*, **3** (1963).

White, Irving S., "The Perception of Value in Products," in Joseph W. Newman (editor), *On Knowing the Consumer*. New York: John Wiley, 1966, 90–108.

Willett, Ronald P., and David T. Kollatt, "Impulse Purchasing as a Special Case of Consumer Decision Making," in L. George Smith (editor), *Reflections on Progress in Marketing*. Chicago: American Marketing Association, 1964.

Wilson, Clark L., "Homemaker Living Patterns and Marketplace Behavior," in John S. Wright and Jac L. Goldstucker (editors), *New Ideas for Successful Marketing*. Chicago: American Marketing Association, 1966, 305–331.

Woods, Walter A., "Psychological Dimensions of Consumer Decisions," *Journal of Marketing*, **24** (January 1960), 15–19.

Yoell, William A., "Determination of Consumer Attitudes and Concepts Through Behavioral Analysis," in Lee Adler and Irving Crespi (editors), *Attitude Research at Sea*. Chicago: American Marketing Association, 1966, 15–28.

Zajonc, R. B., and J. Morrisett, "Cognitive Behavior Under Uncertainty and Ambiguity," *Psychological Reports*, **6** (1960), 31–36.

Zimbardo, Phillip G., "Involvement and Communication Discrepancy as Determinants of Opinion Conformity," *Journal of Abnormal and Social Psychology*, **60** (1960), 86–94.

Index